The Poor Have Faces

The
Poor
Have Faces

Loving Your Neighbor in the 21st Century

John and Sylvia Ronsvalle

BAKER BOOK HOUSE
Grand Rapids, Michigan 49516

© 1991, 1992 by
empty tomb, ® *inc.*

First edition published 1992 by Baker Books
a division of Baker Book House Company
P.O. Box 6287, Grand Rapids, MI 49516-6287

Second printing, April 1996

Printed in the United States of America

Library of Congress Cataloging-in-Publication Data

Ronsvalle, John.
    The poor have faces : loving your neighbor in the twenty-first century / John Ronsvalle and Sylvia Ronsvalle.
       p. cm.
    Includes bibliographical references.
    ISBN 0-8010-7764-8
    1. Church work with the poor. 2. Poverty—Religious aspects—Christianity. 3. Church and social problems. 4. Ronsvalle, John. 5. Ronsvalle, Sylvia. I. Ronsvalle, Sylvia. II. Title.
BV639.P6R66 1992
261.8'3456—dc20   92-916

For the children
in hope

Contents

Preface

$\mathcal{W}$hen we have visited some African-American churches, people who gave testimonies often began with the words, "Giving honor to God, . . ."

This approach always struck us as particularly appropriate. Therefore, if we may borrow from this tradition, we would like to begin this preface by giving honor to God, and to the Lord Jesus Christ.

On the following pages a global as well as national strategy for caring about our neighbors is discussed. These broader ideas and perspectives have blossomed out of years of local ministry. This book reflects the support that the work of *empty tomb, inc.* has received from the churches in the Champaign-Urbana, Illinois, area over the years. Many different congregations and individuals have participated in this ministry. Some individuals have moved to other parts of the country and the world, and yet stay in touch. Without their involvement, the works through *empty tomb* would be only abstract ideas, rather than practical realities that encouraged us to expand our thinking to the larger possibilities that exist for the church in the United States.

In addition to the strategies discussed, the stories on the following pages describe our attempts to be faithful in cross-cultural experiences. We express our appreciation for those who befriended us when we arrived as foreigners in their home environments. Our neighbors at the housing project where we live, the friends we have made through local outreach activities, the people in Brazil who opened themselves to us, treating us not as strangers but as family, and our friends in China who accepted us, shared with us, and laughed with us, are part of the reason this book now exists.

Two people have been instrumental in bringing this book into being. Mark Fackler showed creative concern for the manuscript and encouraged us over a period of years. Allan Fisher of Baker Book House played a vital role in changing potential into reality.

We hope that the combination of support, encouragement, and inspiration we have received has resulted in a book that points to new possibilities and vision on behalf of the children— red, yellow, black, brown, and white, all the children of the world— whom Jesus loves. It is to them that this book is dedicated.

Introduction

A Unique Call for Our Times

*I*n every age, God has called people to meet the unique challenges of their times.

From Noah to Abraham, from Moses to the prophets, from Sarah to Mary, God called people to fulfill special tasks within their historic settings. The apostles responded to Jesus, and set in motion the movement that would change the world. Paul, the Jewish Roman citizen, was able to take advantage of the newly built road system during an extended time of peace, the *pax Romana,* to carry the Good News far and wide.

In more recent history, our spiritual ancestors have been no less faithful. In the nineteenth century, individuals were willing to board ships for unfamiliar destinations too exotic even to imagine. Leaving homes and security, these pioneers spent their lives planting churches, many of which have matured in our own time. Meanwhile, many great social movement have grown out of the faithfulness of those who stayed behind. Such major cultural advances as the abolition of slavery, the civil rights movement, the improved treatment of the mentally ill and prisoners, and campaigns to end political corruption have been rooted in the efforts of followers of Jesus Christ who were faithful to the call for their time.

To what, then, are Christians in the United States called today?

Some people refer to these times as a post-Christian era. Even so, 37 percent of our population is in a historically Christian congregation on any given Sunday, over 60 percent claims formal membership in a Christian denomination, and one recent survey found that 77 percent of our citizenry believes in heaven.

We live in a highly technical age, where we turn to specialists for everything from physical illnesses to beauty techniques. Many of us are left feeling intimidated by trying to fix even a leaky pipe, for lack of specific training or a particular tool.

Even as previously simple tasks become more complicated for us, we have more information than ever before. The evening news brings world-changing events into our living rooms even as they happen. We not only become more familiar with our neighbors around the globe, but we are expected to develop sophistication about countless different cultures.

Our nation has a longstanding tradition of democracy and freedom of religion, privileges that other societies still clamor for as the 1990s unfold. Yet less than 60 percent of eligible voters cast ballots in our 1988 presidential election. We live in one of the richest societies in the history of the world, with the average citizen living more comfortably than any but the highest classes have in the past. Yet we hear criticisms from others, like one Japanese observer who said that our affluence has made us so complacent that we tolerate mediocrity in our products. We have affluence, information, and freedom—and many of the bad side effects that can come with such success.

Surely God is extending a special call to those of us who are Christians in this society and at this point in history! Should we not examine the purpose for which generations of our ancestors married, birthed, and died? Is there not a unique mission for which God has prepared us through the faithfulness of our spiritual ancestors across the centuries?

Although circumstances change, the call is still the same. Jesus presented his followers with this task: "Therefore go and make disciples of all nations . . . teaching them to obey everything I have commanded you" (Matt. 28:19–20). Our challenge is to understand the responsibility of this Great Commission in the context of our times. Today, few of us feel the need to throw our knapsacks on a ship or plane and say good-bye to our homeland so we can sojourn in some mysterious, unknown land as God's servants. For one thing, there are few truly mysterious places left—given the convenience of travel and the speed of satellite communication systems. For another, the sowing efforts of our forebears in the faith have ripened into churches that are growing and sending out missionaries of their own. Although there are still areas of the world where no church groups are meeting, the majority of us will not have a direct hand in planting those witnessing communities.

Yet we who call ourselves Christians in the latter twentieth century have an opportunity unique in the history of the church. We are in a position to respond to the Great Commission in ways undreamed of by our spiritual ancestors. We have more information than ever before, but we must wade through all the input and develop strategies that help us process it intelligently. We have more resources than ever before, but we must learn how to gain control of this potential and harness it for accomplishing great things in Jesus' name. Through our congregations and denominational structures, we have state-of-the-art ministry channels that can work in partnership with established churches in many other countries and thereby benefit from the specialized understanding and experience of our representatives overseas. The special challenge here is to build bridges between the local congregations and the denominational and paradenominational agencies, so there can be partnership between the local and national church structures in the United States, as well as international ministries that transcend cultural differences.

Meeting these challenges will require many of us to change the way we live, although that is never easy. Even if we already understand the demands of the gospel, it is difficult to sacrifice our personal comfort merely because it is "the right thing to do." This is not meant as criticism, but is merely a statement of fact. As we recognize the truth of our complacency, we need to figure out ways to know our neighbors on a deeper level, both across town and across the seas. When we feel personal concern, we will be more willing to respond in ways that impact the patterns of our daily lives. We will want to help our neighbors in practical ways. Depending on the situation, it may be appropriate to share the gospel with them or to help them with the resources so they can share the gospel with others. On the other hand, they may indicate an immediate priority is to address the physical hardship they face.

In this book, we want to do two things. First, we want to share a few of the cross-cultural adventures we have had. If you have had similar opportunities, these passages may remind you of your own experiences. On the other hand, your life's journey may not have brought you into direct contact with people in other countries and cultures. By sharing our personal history, perhaps you can identify with some of the people we have met and begin to care in deeper ways about these neighbors who were formerly strangers.

Building on this personal caring, our second goal is to give you an overview that frees you to explore your role in God's solution for current world problems. Rather than feeling overwhelmed by the enormity of these needs, we ought to be excited about the picture unfolding before us. We hope you will evaluate the facts we present in light of some of the people you have known or those you will meet in our personal narratives. We hope you will be challenged to a greater understanding of the potential for responding that we in this privileged land have. You can help impact world need in Jesus' name in startling ways, but only if you want to. There has never been a group of Christians with as many resources, as much information, as much freedom, as those of us in the United States now possess. We are writing history through our daily lives. The question is: What kind of part are we crafting for ourselves in this grand saga? We have the opportunity to write a spectacular chapter in the annals of the church if we embrace servanthood in the unique context of the late twentieth century. To be part of what God is accomplishing around the world, we need only respond to his call with as much enthusiasm and courage as so many Christians before us have done.

By God's grace, each of us has a unique contribution to make in Jesus' name as the history of the world unfolds in our time.

I

Bread from Jesus

Learning Firsthand about World Needs

One of the few things we knew for certain about the people of Northeast Brazil was that they needed to build outhouses. Now we were on a plane, going there for a visit. Our sincere hope as the airliner streaked past the equator was that they had been successful in building those outhouses. It had become a very practical consideration for us!

You might think this is a strange thing to know about a foreign land, but to us it was a perfectly logical bit of information. Churches in Champaign County, Illinois, had worked across denominational lines since 1977 on a "second-mile giving project." We had developed a relationship with a Christian agency in Northeast Brazil. Now, in September 1982, we were part of a small delegation going to visit that agency to see what our gifts had helped accomplish over those years.

It Began with an Idea

We had founded and incorporated *empty tomb* in 1970 in Urbana, the seat of Champaign County. The original idea was to provide practical ways for Christians to care about their neighbors in need. By 1976, *empty tomb* was sponsoring an active food delivery system, clothing and furniture distribution, a home-renovation effort, and a monthly dinner to bring Christians together, rich and poor, black and white. Because the response from area Christians was strong, we were very busy.

The theme running through our local works was that *empty tomb* was not organized to "take care of" the poor on behalf of the rich. Rather, we continually emphasized that we were a bridge by which contact could be made between financially secure Christians and those in need. If the people in need were Christians, what better way to encourage them in their faith than to share something practical in Jesus' name? If the person in need was not a Christian, the sharing became a very real demonstration of God's love.

Because we wanted people-to-people contacts established, we organized volunteers to deliver food to needy families in person. Too often, "poverty" is merely an abstract idea; we lose sight of the fact that it is not "statistics" who are hungry, but individuals with names and faces. When volunteers can see specific people going hungry, they more deeply understand the importance of taking action to end that deprivation.

Strong emphasis was placed on meeting people directly in all the works. The goal was to bring people together through the various distribution and renovation projects. For example, to provide a chance for actual friendship and fellowship, the monthly potluck dinners gathered people in an experience that transcended traditional economic and racial barriers. Everyone brought a dish, and as greens and cornbread mingled with avocado salad on our plates, we sat side by side, getting to know each other as friends.

Although we were busy with the needs of our immediate neighbors, we realized we could not ignore the serious needs beyond our community. People were starving in the sub-Saharan region of Africa and facing hunger and other desperate situations from Brazil to Bangladesh. How could our personalized approach be applied to people beyond our local borders? Could Christians in the United States, more specifically in Champaign County, be challenged above and beyond their own denominational mission outreaches to help needy people around the world?

By 1981, twenty-eight congregations were cooperating on a second-mile mission project we called Bread from Jesus. The name came from John 6:35, where Jesus announces, "I am the bread of life." We wanted to declare that whatever help we were able to give, whether bread or building materials, came in Jesus' name. With the physical caregiving, we wanted to offer spiritual hope as well.

We raised an average of $20,000 each year through two kinds of projects. In one, a pastor and a layperson from a congregation would help repair or build a home for a Champaign-Urbana resident. Members of about twenty-five congregations pledged money for the hours their volunteers worked, much like pledges are made for miles walked. That money was designated for use in Brazil. The other community program brought farmers and urban residents together. The urban partner donated the cost of chemicals and seeds for one acre of farmland; the farmer donated the land and the labor. The value of the produce from a dedicated acre was donated to the overseas project.

The money thus raised was sent to Northeast Brazil through a Christian agency called Diaconia. Local enthusiasm for the project was high. It was exciting to see that a group of people working in Champaign County was helping a group of people in Northeast Brazil to impact terrible living conditions in a coordinated fashion. By helping the area year after year, we learned about the problems as they arose and had feedback about what our funds had accomplished. Instead of moving haphazardly from one distant crisis to another, we began to be familiar with the people in this area of the world. As one pastor put it, through this project's structure, "The poor have faces."

By the time of our trip, we had been sending an average annual donation of $17,000 to Northeast Brazil. Diaconia distributed this money and provided information on how it was used. The reports contained financial budgets on specific projects, and also put them in the context of the circumstances in Brazil, giving us an overview of conditions there. They shared individual stories and included photographs of the progress being made.

From the beginning, we had communicated to Diaconia that we wanted to follow their lead on the types of projects needed in Brazil. The agency was very willing to share end-use information (how donations are used at the receiving end) with us. The annual reports we received accounted for the money, provided descriptions of the various projects, and included a personal message from Diether Jäckel, then superintendent of Diaconia for the North/Northeast, and now General Secretary for the national organization. From these reports, we learned about the drought cycle that ravaged this area. We learned of the subsistence farming that often drove people to the cities to live in *favelas,* or slums, often built on garbage dumps or swamps. We learned that water cisterns and outhouses built by local workers with Diaconia's assistance were helping to prevent diseases caused by poor sanitation.

These reports were informative, but Diether Jäckel wrote that it would be so much more enlightening if some people from our area could come to Brazil and see the results firsthand. In the sixth year of the effort, four of us went to meet our distant friends in Diaconia and see just what our financial gifts had helped accomplish.

Recife, Pernambuco State, Brazil

We wondered what we would see in this tropical place, so different from central Illinois. As it turned out, we landed in the very cosmopolitan city of Recife, which has a population of two million. Its tall modern buildings contrasted sharply with classic Portuguese architecture, but our first impression was of a bustle of cars leaving the crowded airport. Since the terminal had open-air grillwork between the walls and the roof, our first thought was, "How impractical!—what do they do when it snows?" Ah, came the amused second thought, snow was not likely here, one hundred miles south of the equator.

We learned right away, though, that warm equatorial breezes and open-air buildings were not the only differences we would experience. The person driving turned to us as we approached a red traffic light. "Ah, I must explain. I am not going to stop at this light," he said in his heavily accented English. We must have looked surprised and worried, because he went on, slightly apologetically, "We never stop at red traffic lights at night. This is one of the realities of living in a city where seventy percent of the people are poor. To stop is an invitation for robbery."

We looked out the window into the tropical night, which suddenly seemed threatening. As the buildings sped by, we guessed that the decorative iron grillwork on the windows and doors served a security purpose as well.

While in the city we chose to stay at a Catholic orphanage rather than a hotel. The hundred little girls were charming and the head nun made us feel like special guests. She told us that the orphanages could house only a small percentage of the hundred thousand abandoned children in Recife. So, four-, five-, and six-year-olds for whom there was no room in the orphanages formed gangs to beg or steal and slept under bridges or in doorways.

Didn't the parents care about their children? How could these little ones be on their own? Diaconia staff explained the difficulties of life in Northeast Brazil. Drought often makes it impossible for rural parents to raise enough food, even for just the family. Although people in outlying villages have various reasons for coming to the city, most often the parents of these homeless children had left the countryside to find work in the city, only to discover that the rumors of urban jobs and success were unfounded.

The disappointed family then must put up a cardboard hut, adding on to one of the *favelas* on a vacant lot or an old garbage dump. While the father looks for work, the mother tries to take in washing. The parents hope to exchange cardboard for wood pieces and make the house more permanent and comfortable. Finally the father goes to work in the sugarcane fields or walks two thousand miles to the industrialized South. In either case, he may be gone for months or years. He will try to earn money to bring back to his family, but the work is very hard and he may break his health before making enough to support his wife and children.

Life in Northeast Brazil is hard, whether in a city or a rural area. The 1980 census had been conducted two years before our visit. Reports based on that data indicated that the average life span in that region was only 52.6 years, as opposed to 60.0

years nationwide. In the rural area of one northeastern state, men could expect to live only 43.3 years.[1]

With the father away, the mother is left to raise the family alone. We asked our hosts if it was true that Brazil has a "macho" culture. Yes, we were told. Even churchgoing men, whether Protestant or Catholic, may have a girlfriend in addition to a wife. If the man helps support a second family, it is even seen as a kind of social-welfare effort. A boyfriend's gifts help the mother, but as new babies are born, a child as young as four may wander away. Then the child either can't find home again or learns that the streets provide some reward, as long as one doesn't get caught.

Because many Northeasterners are fiercely loyal to their small rural farms, leaving them takes a great crisis. Still, necessity forces many to do so. Sometimes, legal technicalities allow larger landholders to buy a small farm one family has worked for generations. Or crop failure and resulting debts cost a family their farm. Maybe a young man starts a family but finds no place on his parents' five acres for him and his older brothers' families. Maybe the hope of better conditions, electricity, or job opportunities lure him away. Too often, it is not gold but *favelas* that wait at the end of Rainbow Road.

That is why, the Diaconia staff told us, a lot of the organization's energy is spent on improving living conditions in the interior. Seeds help to replant after crop failures. Wells and cisterns allow survival during droughts. Health clinics mean that simple illnesses no longer are fatal.

We were anxious to visit the rural villages where our funds had made a difference.

Scenes from the Interior

We have left Recife miles behind us. After a ride on dusty, bumpy one-lane roads, we move into a three-room house with a local Brazilian Mennonite volunteer. She will be our hostess as we visit this small rural village.

Now we walk down one hill and up another. What a leisure culture we have in flat Illinois! Here, in rural Northeast Brazil, even the simplest tasks—getting water or fuel for the day, working the land, visiting people—absorb a surprising amount of time and energy.

After a few minutes of trying not to slip down one particularly steep hill, we no longer think about our red faces, hard breathing, and the sweat that rolls down our cheeks. All our concentration is bent on securing a firm footing. Bare feet would have fit into the toeholds easier that our boots, but bare feet would also have made us vulnerable to parasites.

One hundred miles to the west there is a desert between us and the Amazon jungle. Here, so close to the coast, plants still grow quickly. Palm and banana trees, and other plants that are hard to guess about, crowd the earth. Most farmers hack out a half-acre on a hillside and plant rows up and down the hill. The Mennonite missionaries in this area have said they have tried to convince people to terrace across the slopes, but because of the difficulty of cutting terraces into the steep hills by hand, few farmers adopt the new method.

At the top of a hill is a community center, but no teacher comes here anymore. Although the government constructed the building, the local farmers cannot afford to pay a teacher's salary. The children in this village who do go to school walk four miles each way. Many children cannot go because they must help in the family's field. Also, since uniforms and school supplies are required, a family may have trouble supplying these for more than one child at a time. Even the most basic education costs more than these families can afford.

The former school now stands empty except when used for meetings. This day, our Mennonite hostess is teaching a weekly health class. The ladies come, dressed in clean cotton, although laundry is done by hand, often on rocks, and may take one or more days a week. Bleach and sun-drying kill the bacteria in the water.

The ladies laugh and talk and look shyly at us. It is apparently exciting to have foreign visitors attend their class. Today the lesson is on dehydration in babies.

Probably none of these ladies have ever been out of the village. It is hard to guess how old they are—they all seem ageless, not quite young on the way to being very old. It is strange to look at the ladies, knowing that of thirty-five families in this area, close to half have experienced the death of four or more children. Probably most died of easily preventable or curable infectious or parasitic diseases.[2]

When Diaconia first came to this area, a staff person asked the men of the village what kind of help they would like. The men talked it over and came back with one request—"Please help our children to stop dying." That is how the sanitation project began.

Today the Mennonite missionary explains that the baby's soft spot sinks in when the baby is dehydrated. One lady comments, "Oh, that happened to my baby in the morning and she was dead at night." The other women nod in understanding.

After an evening meal of potatoes with a local family, it is time to go to the rosary service, held every night in October. At various homes, people gather to read the Bible, to reflect on what it means for their lives, and to say the rosary. Since the priest is able to visit the *sitio* (village) only once a month, lay leaders are responsible for the service the rest of the time. People come from miles away, up and down the hilly footpaths. We carefully trace a dark path. The way seems endless, when suddenly a house appears, light streaming from its windows.

We enter an 8-by-10 room. At one end a picture of Jesus is surrounded by twenty candles. Benches and chairs line the walls. Brazilian hospitality dictates that the visitors sit in chairs facing the picture of Jesus across the room, while others stand. The young men gather toward the rear corner of the room, to our right, while the young women stand in the middle of the room, their backs to the men and us. Older people sit or stand in every other foot of space. Many people are on the porch, looking in the windows. We each take a child on our laps. How slight they seem for six or seven or eight years old. One shy little girl looks up with a pretty smile, her eyes permanently crossed.

The service begins with a reading from the Portuguese translation of *Good News for Modern Man*. Tonight's passage is the Sermon on the Mount, Matthew 6. After the rosary is said, some verses are read again.

Antonio is the leader. He has a smiling, tanned face and a slim body, firm from the physical labor on his farm. Antonio has a calm authority about him. In a conversation after the meeting, Antonio tells us he has his son read the Bible to him regularly. He recognizes, he says, that Jesus' teaching of God's love for all people, no matter how poor, is very good news. And he wants to share it with others.

"What do these verses in Matthew mean for us?" Antonio asks those at the service. Several people make comments. Then Antonio speaks again: "It seems that if people with money were to give it to people without money, the world would believe in Jesus, because only the Holy Spirit could accomplish that." He looks at his friends and neighbors earnestly and continues: "Those of us with extra must share with the father who cannot feed his children. Unless we share, that father might think God has not provided for him and be tempted into disbelief. We must safeguard his faith."

Antonio has ten children and about five acres of land. His face lights up when he talks of God's goodness and the hope it gives him.

At another village we see more cisterns that our funds have helped to build. We walk a half-mile down a path to see a family breaking apart stones at a pond. The stones will be used to make concrete for their cistern. Most of the labor is provided by each family on its own. The cisterns will be helpful—if rain comes. The hope is always that the rainy season, which lasts for several weeks in years when it comes, will fill the cistern for the following year.

Water can be purchased but is expensive. One person tells us he had bought water from the mayor, only to find it was salty and unusable. If family members have to depend on ponds for their water, they are vulnerable to the risky weather. During the rainy season, there may be usable ponds only a quarter of a mile away. When the dry season begins, the ponds dry up and the family then has to walk farther and farther to find any water. More and more people would be dependent on the limited water available. Cisterns have provided some relief.

We ask a local community leader, who organized the cistern project in cooperation with Diaconia and Mennonite Central Committee volunteers, what would be the next step, now that most of the families have access to water and outhouses. "Land" is his quick response. While rich landowners might own large tracts of land that are uncultivated, many small farmers try to make a subsistence living on ten acres or less. Land is a main issue, our staff guide explains. The rich who own the land, or know those who do, refer to the whole issue as "the social problem"—what to do with all these poor people who don't have land. Apparently both the rich and the poor agree there must be change, but no one has found an acceptable solution.

"Can this issue be settled by peaceful change?" we asked. "If there's enough time," is the response, "and the people are patient enough. No one knows. The children are dying today."

Strategies for Change

Although we did not envy the challenge that Diaconia faced in meeting these needs, we respected the hope and initiative that these staff people brought to the task. Sometimes met with suspicion by the affluent people in their society ("Why would educated people want to help the poor? Are they trying to make trouble for all of us?"), these dedicated Christians are constantly trying to improve life for other Brazilians.

Over the two weeks we were there, we spent several hours talking with the superintendent, Diether Jäckel. We came away with two important insights.

First, as we sat around a table, our delegation began to share our hopes and expectations for the projects we were helping to fund. We talked about the idea of sharing Bibles, which the administrator thought was a good idea and promised to pursue. We also asked for his suggestions about the problem of inflation and how it affects the transfer of funds.

Then we began to explore our hope for a relationship with one particular community or county in Northeast Brazil. We hoped to learn about the general needs in Brazil by developing an understanding with a group of people in one specific area.

Diether Jäckel responded that our financial gifts would be too much for one county to handle. His point was that sharing too much money too quickly in one area would discourage initiative on the part of people there. He was also concerned that other communities would be jealous. Finally, he noted that Diaconia's strategy was to assist a number of projects in different areas, encouraging local leadership rather than running and funding the projects completely.

Of course, his views made sense to us, but this news was still a disappointment. We had hoped that our sharing would involve the exchange of photos and letters so we would get to know specific individuals on a personal level. The challenge, from our point of view, was to convince folks back home to care about these strangers in need. We knew that our efforts must compete with an advertising industry that promotes using all one's money to secure a comfortable lifestyle for oneself. We felt the need for powerful tools that could effectively demonstrate the value of using money for others.

While we continued to discuss this idea, Diether Jäckel was writing something on a notepad. As we talked, we noticed that he wrote two words in English, in capital letters. We read them upside down. Although he never brought them up in the conversation, they spoke very loudly. The words were TRUST and RISK.

We suddenly realized that we had come from the cornfields of Illinois with specific hopes and dreams for this project but little real understanding of the factors involved. It was essential that we address our need for information. We knew that Christians back in Illinois had to have powerful reasons to resist spending money on themselves and instead send funds for people thousands of miles away. We had a good sense of what would most effectively motivate those contributors. We had been providing some money, which gave us a certain amount of influence and power, but if we did not have specific information about how it would be used, we might not be able to raise additional funds. How should we weigh our desire for information against the needs and hopes that Diether Jäckel and Diaconia's staff had for the work in Brazil? Should we emphasize and even insist on projects we knew would appeal to the folks back in Illinois, justifying our actions because we believed it would help raise money and thus help more people?

Or should we *trust* these Brazilian brothers and sisters in Christ and *risk* ourselves in a submitted relationship to them? Diaconia personnel had already proved, through their reports and the projects we had seen, that they were responsible and dependable administrators. We had to decide whether to submit ourselves now to their leadership and develop our fund-raising strategy in light of this submission. We would have to hope that doing it their way could be just as productive as doing it our way. *Trust* and *risk*. As Christians we were being called to a higher order of conducting the project. And we accepted the call.

As the conversations continued over the next few days, we learned a second important insight. Diether Jäckel explained that the northeastern region of Brazil was getting a lot of funding in 1982 because it was experiencing a terrible drought. Whenever a major crisis like this develops, funding is plentiful, since the attention of wealthier nations is directed to the area. However, when the current drought lessened and the rains came, that funding might dry up. If the sub-Saharan region, for example, were to be in crisis again (as, in fact, it was in the mid-80s), the attention, and the funds, of potential contributors would be focused there.

Jäckel was not begrudging aid to other areas. But the possibility of a change in focus meant that Diaconia and similar groups were limited in their approach. Although they certainly could provide emergency relief, it was difficult to take the initiative in planning solutions that would go to the core of the long-term problems. If Diaconia could be sure of receiving funds on a continuing basis, they could be more confident of follow-through and design projects that work at the root causes of the area's poverty, rather than just responding to symptoms. When a crisis arose, it would not be a choice of either meeting the crisis needs or continuing to work out an overall plan. Instead, there would be sufficient funds to apply to the emergency while laying a solid foundation for a better life after the crisis was dealt with.

A Continuing Relationship

We returned to Illinois changed for the better. Maybe at some level we had felt that it was *our* responsibility to understand and straighten out Brazil's problems in this two-week trip. At least we came back relieved. Although we were now aware that the problems were much deeper than anything we could solve on our own, we had a new confidence that there were Brazilian Christians addressing those concerns much better than we could.

We continue to send funds on a regular basis and to receive valuable end-use information from our friends in Northeast Brazil. We were really touched, for example, when we received a tape, with translation, from Diaconia.[3] It was an interview with a community worker, Inez, who tried to help people in one of the *favelas*. Her comments warmed our hearts. At first she described conditions in the *favela* during the drought:

> In times past this place used to be the city dump and these poor children, mainly the older ones, picked garbage in the dump. The truck would come from its pick-up and deposit trash here—the worst, foulest stuff in the world, covered with vultures. There were all sorts of repulsive things: dead dogs,

dead animals and all sorts of other things, and these children, barefoot, were always there. . . .

Inez said that during the drought, many children had died of starvation. The fathers would grieve because there was nothing they could do to get food for their family.

It was very sad here at that time because if one were to come to the center of this very street where we are now, you could see the *urubu* [scavenger birds] on the trash pile, and the children going through the trash in search of a crust of bread that they might find to eat. . . . The birds would come around the children who would throw rocks at them so that they, the children, could have the scraps that might be found.

How meaningful, then, to read that Inez felt that "it was the greatest happiness" that she ever felt when Diaconia came to offer help to this community. Our funds allowed Diaconia to work with this group, not only to meet the immediate crisis, but to begin dealing with some of the foundational problems in the community.

And for me, just talking with you about it now, makes me very happy within as I remember that sad time and how happy a day it was when Diaconia brought that great, great help that was from Bread from Jesus. Just talking to you about it brings emotions to a peak so that I cannot contain myself to express further all that happened. I already feel a squeeze on my heart.

Inez then described the projects that had gone beyond immediate needs. For example, houses began to be built as more permanent dwellings: "Thanks to God, all of those people today are really going ahead, full strength; they used to be hungry—you would have to see to believe it; but they worked joyfully and in the end, thanks to God, with this work force group, they made many bricks and built the houses and covered them with tile."

Although acknowledging there is still great need in the *favela,* she concluded:

> I want to thank you very much, mainly for the help we had from Diaconia which was great and also from the brethren who came from so far, through Bread from Jesus, who helped us very much. I ask of God, of Jesus Christ, that he pour out great blessings on each and all; this is what I desire from the bottom of my heart.

How much our limited help was able to accomplish! Reports like these are a great encouragement to continue our efforts to relate to the people in Northeast Brazil. We are certainly not ending all world hunger, but it is clear that our small gifts are making a difference in these people's lives. Too often the needs in the world seem so overwhelming that we wonder if it is possible to make any difference. True, everything can't be solved at once—but our project has shown that we have helped our brothers and sisters in one area of the world.

Our stewardship research has convinced us that we Christians have the means to help others as never before in history. What if Christians in other areas of the United States each took a part in addressing world need? Certainly we could have a far greater impact on evangelization and hunger than we have up to now.

This kind of thinking has led us to some interesting possibilities. . . .

2

Abounding Grace

Exploring Mission Resources

$\mathscr{A}$lthough the conditions in Brazil are terrible indeed, the sadder truth is that people face such hard lives in many parts of the world. For those of us who live in the United States, the reality of what these people face is almost too difficult to think about. Therefore, it might be helpful to explore this idea a little further.

Take a piece of paper and write down one word that describes your feelings after reading the following facts:

Worldwide, 38,000 children, five years old and under, die each day from preventable poverty conditions.[1]

Between 1700 and 1987, there have been 471 wars, in which 101,550,000 people were killed.[2] In the past ten years alone, at least 136,000,000 children have died from preventable poverty conditions—more children in ten years than all the people in all the wars in 287 years.[3]

For every one child who dies in poverty, six more will live on, permanently damaged by the deprivations they have faced.[4] For example, each day 500 children become permanently blind for lack of vitamin A.[5]

Although the Good News of Jesus has been around for almost two thousand years, it is estimated that one-quarter to one-half of the earth's population has not had a chance to hear the gospel message. Projects to evangelize the entire world by the year 2000 are blossoming, but one survey concluded that this effort will probably fail—at least in part because of underfunding.[6]

Now pause a moment. Write down your reaction. What emotion swells to the surface of your consciousness? What word summarizes your feelings?

Was it "anger"? Or "despair"? Or "defeat"?

If you felt those emotions, you are not alone. In their book *Compassion,* Henri Nouwen, Donald McNeill, and Douglas Morrison suggest that it is not true that church members do not care or do not know enough about world conditions. In fact, we have more information than ever before. Through television and magazines, church mission channels and materials, people have so much information that many of them feel overwhelmed and probably angry about their inability to impact these desperate needs. And so, numbness sets in, as a kind of defense mechanism that protects them from conditions they feel they can't change.[7]

Our own experience is that church members care very deeply about others. For twenty years we have worked with volunteers from many different churches. These folks have delivered food to public-housing projects, given up Saturday mornings to repair a stranger's home, donated and sorted clothes, and delivered furniture. Many Christians we know have been eager to do all kinds of projects to help others—when the goals were clear, and they understood how their actions can bring about a change for the better.

We are convinced that church members *want* to make a difference. Before we consider how Christians in the United States can best use their resources to help others, we must first address a more basic question. That is, do church members actually have the means to impact such dramatic needs as those that exist in our own country and overseas?

Hope for the Overwhelmed

Reading the Bible is always informative and often surprising. For example, there is an interesting verse in 2 Corinthians 9:8: "And God is able to make all grace abound to you, so that in all things at all times, having all that you need, you will abound in every good work."

This verse contains an important promise. In a study of world conditions, one can't help but be touched by the enormous needs that become evident. After singing "Jesus loves the little children, all the children of the world!" for so many years in Sunday school, any Christian knows that Jesus' heart is grieving to see so many children in pain around the globe. Certainly, helping children in desperate poverty or telling people how much God loves them qualifies as a "good work." But if it is God's will that we "abound" in such activities, where are the resources he promises? This question was the basis of the stewardship study that follows. Could 2 Corinthians 9:8 be believed as a principle for our times?

The answer may surprise you. In regard to the United States, one might conclude that God has indeed kept his part of the bargain to provide all that we need. Americans in general, including many Christians, are some of the wealthiest people in the history of the world. We are living in a unique period of the human story. Until quite recently, most people in every society were struggling for survival. It was only a minority that could meet the basic need for food, clothing, and shelter and have extra money besides. A much larger percentage earned just enough to make ends meet, and many could not even manage that.

After World War II, the world economy improved in many regions. In Europe, North America, Japan, Australia, and New Zealand, more and more people had better standards of living. For example, for the first time most people in the United States had enough to meet their basic needs, plus money left over. "Discretionary income" became a reality for the majority. But those who now could provide for themselves and their families faced a new kind of question that few had been able to ask before: What should we do with our surplus?

Per-capita, or per person, income in this country has been growing steadily since World War II. "Disposable personal income" refers to income after taxes. By converting the figures to 1982 dollars, we can compare the amounts in "constant dollars," dollars converted to a base value that is adjusted for inflation. Per-capita disposable personal income increased in the 1920s. There was a serious dip during the Great Depression, and then an artificial high during World War II. After the war, individual income began to rise, and it continued to do so in the decades that followed.

It would seem, then, that financial resources have been increasingly available to most of us throughout this century. If God has provided all that we need, has the second part of the formula outlined in 2 Corinthians 9:8 come true? Do believers in America "abound in every good work"?

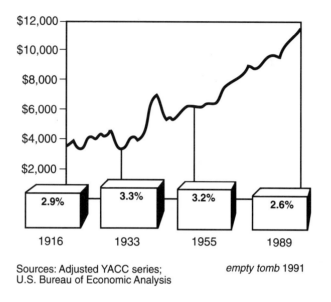

Sources: Adjusted YACC series;   *empty tomb* 1991
U.S. Bureau of Economic Analysis

Figure 1. Protestant Giving as a Percentage of Income, 1916, 1933, 1955 and 1989 Contrasted with U.S. Per Capita Disposable Personal Income, 1916–1989, in Constant 1982 Dollars.[8]

Analyzing church giving patterns took on a new dimension during this period of rising incomes. Did church members increase their benevolence as they became richer? Data for Protestants from about 1916 through the present is available to help answer that question.

In 1916, the year before we entered World War I, Protestants in the United States gave an average of 2.9 percent of their income to their churches. In 1933, the deepest point of the Great Depression, Protestants gave 3.3 percent of their income to their churches. By 1955, the percentage given to church was again a little more than 3 percent. However, since the 1960s, while American incomes have risen steadily, giving by church members has taken up a decreasing proportion of those incomes. Although the average American is over 200 percent

richer than in 1933, the percentage of income given to church
had shrunk from 3.3 percent to 2.6 percent in 1989, a percentage *decrease* of over 20 percent from the 1933 base. (See fig. 1.)

A 1991 study explored giving patterns in a variety of
Protestant denominations in 1968 and 1985–1989.[9] This
study's findings look similar to the broader patterns just outlined. In a composite of thirty-one of the denominations, giving expressed as a percentage of income in 1985 compared to
the 1968 base decreased by 8.5 percent while per-capita
income had increased by 31 percent between 1968 and 1985.
In the period 1985–1989, giving as a percentage of income
continued to decline.

This pattern held true regardless of the theological perspective of the denominations studied. Nine of the denominations
studied belonged to the National Council of the Churches of
Christ in the U.S.A. (NCC), while seven belonged to the
National Association of Evangelicals (NAE). The NAE denominations received a higher percentage of their members'
incomes than the NCC denominations during the period studied. However, the NAE denominations experienced a faster
decline in the percent of income that members were giving. In
1968, the NCC churches were receiving 3.1 percent of their
members' incomes. By 1985, this had decreased to 2.7 percent.
On the other hand, the NAE denominations were receiving 6.8
percent of members' incomes in 1968. In 1985, these denominations were receiving an average of 5.2 percent of members'
incomes. By 1989, the same nine NCC denominations were
receiving 2.9 percent of their members' income while six of the
original seven NAE denominations were receiving 4.7 percent.

We must conclude that—although most people in the
United States have had more and more resources available to
them as the century has unfolded, there has not been a similar

increase in their giving to churches. If we have so much more to spend, and it is not going into the church, where is it going?

"Great Expectations"

Many of us may resist the notion that we are actually "richer" than ever before. At the end of the month, the checkbook may show a zero balance. There are so many things we want that we can't afford. If we are so much richer, why don't we feel richer?

It may well be that the one thing that has grown faster than our incomes is our expectations. What used to be considered luxuries we now regard as necessities. For example, *Fortune* magazine, in a cover story, suggested that people who want to buy a first home are having trouble—not because they can't afford *a* house, but because they want to start with a house as nice as their parents ended up with. In fact, if a young couple today bought a house similar to a starter home of twenty-five years ago, it would be comparable to a mobile home. However, it would have more luxuries and would be housing fewer people per square foot, and it would still cost half what it cost their parents.[10] At least in the case of obtaining "adequate" housing, our expectations may be just as big a limiting factor as income.

Look at spending patterns from another perspective. The year 1987 is the latest year for which a broad-based estimate of income is available for North American Protestant overseas ministries. This figure includes denominational programs, interdenominational groups such as World Relief of the NAE and Church World Service of the NCC, and such para-denominational groups as World Vision. The budgets for all these overseas ministries totaled $1.7 billion.[11] It is reasonable to estimate that Catholic contributions for overseas programs would not increase this amount beyond $2 billion.[12]

Compare this figure of $2 billion to help people overseas with what Americans buy for themselves in a given year. In 1985, Americans spent $3.5 billion on cut flowers; the pet industry (including restaurants, insurance, and dentistry) collected an estimated $8 billion. In 1987, women's sheer hosiery commanded $3.5 billion, while golf equipment racked up $2 billion in sales. And video games! The kind that gulp quarters at arcades garnered $2.9 billion, while pinball machines consumed $2.6 billion. Although one brand of home video games now on the market did not even exist in 1986, sales soared to $1.7 billion in 1987. While people around the world struggle to find enough to eat for children who may suffer permanent brain damage from poor nutrition, Americans in 1988 supported a diet industry to the tune of $29 billion and spent $12 billion on candy. In 1989, sales of soft drinks totaled $44 billion. (See table 1 at the end of this chapter.)

One elderly saint, hearing these statistics, said indignantly, "Those are not *churched* children putting quarters into video game machines!" For the sake of argument, let's say that most of them are not. Consider the fact, then, that unchurched children in this country have more quarters for video games than all the churched adults in the country have dollars for international church ministries. It is certainly true that church members are only one segment of our population. Approximately 37 percent are in a church with a historic Christian confession on any given Sunday morning,[13] while others attend less frequently or on special occasions. That means only a portion of the approximately 68 percent of the United States population that *claims* membership in historically Christian churches[14] is actively participating in a local congregation on a regular basis. Still, for purposes of comparison, we can see that while our money is flowing freely into a variety of leisure and luxury industries, a relatively low level of support exists for international ministries.

A more personal commentary on the expectation factor was provided by Levi Keidel, who served as a career missionary through the Mennonite Church in Zaire, Africa. He first went overseas just when Americans began to have more resources beyond their immediate needs. He reflected on what it was like to be away from home during this period and return on furlough every so often:

> But I remember when we first came home on our furlough in 1955, number one furlough. The status symbols at that time were a black and white television, and wall-to-wall carpeting in the living room.
>
> Five years later, it was color TV and automatic washers and dryers.
>
> Come back on furlough number three: it was dishwashers and stereo sound systems.
>
> Come back on furlough number four: recreation vehicles, backyard swimming pools.
>
> Come back now on furlough five: video cameras, satellite dishes, personal computers.[15]

Yes, we have "great expectations" for ourselves—more conveniences, more luxuries in our daily lives. But it is important to ask ourselves which of the expenditures listed in the table on pages 53–54 are actually sinful. Which are contradictory to what we learn in the Bible about the Christian lifestyle? If we study the table, we would have to conclude that although few of the purchases are necessarily bad, these expenditures become obscene and offensive when contrasted with the figure for ministry support. If enjoying our luxuries becomes more important to us than giving support to the work of the church, the pursuit of pleasure has taken precedence over our love for God and our dedication to the work of his kingdom. We are then in danger of having the seeds of the Good News that were sown in our hearts choked out by "the worries of this life and the deceitfulness of wealth" (Matt. 13:22).

At this point in the discussion, you might be wondering about other "charitable" giving. Perhaps, the thinking often goes, we are giving less to our churches and more to other charities. If that were true, that would account for the decreased percentage of income given to churches. Are people as generous as before but directing their giving elsewhere?

In terms of "religious" giving, the trend for all religions seems to match the slight decline noted in the 1988 study of Protestants. In terms of giving to nonreligious charities, a national effort is currently being conducted to obtain a more reliable estimate of total charitable giving. However, a review of data presently available does not suggest that nonreligious charities are receiving more income at the expense of churches. One estimate for religious giving to paradenominational groups beyond the congregation suggests that individuals give 90 percent of their contributions through their congregation, with the remainder going to groups outside the congregation.[16] And even before the recent decline in contributions to the televangelists, these electronic ministries did not account for more than about 2 percent of total religious giving to historically Christian activities.[17]

The sad truth seems to be that, as Americans have become richer, their charitable efforts have become a smaller and smaller portion of their total lives.

How Much Is Enough?

Okay, so we have begun to understand that we have been slacking off in terms of sharing. Suppose now that church members in the United States were willing to increase their giving to the church. Suppose that these same church members were concerned about the level of support for international ministries and might be willing to consider an increase in giving *if they thought it would help*. It would be hard to forgo certain comforts, but church members might do so if properly informed. However, they would want to know that their change in lifestyle was worth it. If people spend less on pets and video and movies and sports equipment and begin to earmark more of their surplus to help others in need, will it actually do any good? We need to look at how much it would take to make a significant dent in world need.

Here is more good news! The best estimate available suggests that $30 to $50 billion a year could meet the most essential human needs around the world.[18] Projects for clean water and sanitation, prenatal and infant/maternal care, basic education, immunizations, and long-term development efforts are among the activities that could help overcome the poverty conditions that now kill and maim so many children and adults.

That figure of $30 to $50 billion may sound like anything but good news. God may be generous, you may agree, but has he been *that* generous? Consider this: If church members in the United States would increase their giving to 10 percent of their income, there would be more than $65 billion per year available for overseas ministries and $15 billion a year for meeting the needs of our neighbors across town, even while maintaining current congregational programs, including building projects. The entire budget of most congregations is being supported by a relatively small portion of their members' incomes. That leaves a lot of potential for increased giving, which would have a major impact on world needs, both physical and spiritual.

It would seem that, yes, 2 Corinthians 9:8 *is* relevant today. God has promised enough resources, and Christians in the United States are receiving more than enough. If we choose to do so, these resources can be directed in creative ways, and we could indeed "abound in every good work." It is within our ability to impact the very distressing needs that seemed so overwhelming at the beginning of this chapter! And the strategy for marshaling the resources is as old as Genesis.

Tithing—Then and Now

We first meet the idea of tithing in Genesis 14:18–20, which tells how Abraham presented "a tenth of everything" to Melchizedek, king of Salem and priest of God Most High, whom Abraham met in the wilderness. Jacob continued the tithe as a spontaneous outpouring of worship (Gen. 28:22), but it was not actually commanded until Moses announced it in Leviticus 27:30. The value God placed on tithing can be seen in the fact that God's wrath was announced on the Israelites by Malachi because they refused to honor this command. Malachi proclaimed that God feels robbed by the people who do not share one-tenth (Mal. 3:6–12).

Jesus did not discredit the tithe. On the contrary, he commended the Pharisees for tithing even down to their spices, although he denounced them for ignoring such important qualities as justice, mercy, and faithfulness: "You should have practiced the latter, *without neglecting the former*" (Matt. 23:23, italics added). Jesus declared that he came not to destroy the law but to fulfill it (Matt. 5:17). These obligations are not burdens but helpful guidelines that allow us to serve and love God more confidently. The tithe, as well as other such practical aids, become instruments of our deepening discipleship, as we join with King David in adoration: "I have hidden your word in my heart, that I might not sin against you" (Ps. 119:11).

In the new covenant, Jesus' disciples are free to begin with the law and then allow their love for God to take them to new levels of love for one another. Thus, we not only should not murder, but even angry thoughts are considered grounds for judgment (Matt. 5:22). We not only must love our friends, but also our enemies (Matt. 5:43–48). We not only should tithe, but we have an even greater challenge as Jesus says, "Sell your possessions and give to the poor" (Luke 12:33). Note that when Jesus speaks these words in Luke 12, he is not talking to "the rich young ruler" but is addressing a crowd. This pronouncement is followed by a parable about being a wise manager because the master may return at any time (Luke 12:35–46). Peter asks if the parable is only for the select disciples or for everyone (v. 41). Jesus clearly implies that it is for anyone who would be considered a worthy servant by the master.

There is little evidence that selling all one's possessions became common among Christians in the early church. Rather, Paul outlined a procedure for proportionate giving that can serve as a model, even today (1 Cor. 16:1–4).

Gifts to the early church were initially needed for "the relief of the sick and poor, the support of the apostles and other traveling missionaries," and the expenses of the public meetings. Believers provided voluntary offerings, giving of firstfruits, tithes, and endowments that resulted from the contribution of land, either donated directly or sold and the proceeds donated.[19] Apparently the tithe fell into disuse, because writers such as Jerome, Ambrose of Milan, and Augustine wrote arguments to support its re-implementation in the fourth century.

By A.D. 585, however, the tithe was already seen as an "ancient custom." In that year, the second Council of Mâcon passed a canon that provided the first sanction for the failure of a church member to tithe—that person would be excommunicated![20] By the Middle Ages, the tithe was forcefully extracted from church members and leaders alike.[21] Originally, church representatives would accompany priests to collect these (in)voluntary gifts. However, as church and state became more closely intertwined, secular soldiers would join the church representatives on their collection rounds. Resentment grew over this practice and even resulted in "tithe wars" in England.[22] The Reformation saw rebellions in direct response to compulsory tithing, but enforcement was continued throughout many European countries.

Even in the New World, where the principle of freeing religion from state intervention was theoretically affirmed, it was by no means a given that such practices would not continue.[23] In fact, laws were on the books for state support of pastors in Connecticut until 1818 and in Massachusetts until 1834. In the Virginia Colony, every male aged sixteen and above was taxed a certain amount of tobacco for the support of the pastor. In geographical areas where a particular church held sway, taxation for church support was more likely. However, with the advent of Methodism and other confessions that rejected the notion of having only one denomination in a given region, a variety of different churches began to emerge in certain colonies. Soon the taxes became impractical, since no denomination was clearly dominant. Without structural enforcement, tithing lost ground as a stewardship practice.

The church in this country has been struggling to find a practical means of support for its work ever since the enforced tithe ended. Lotteries were used for a while. Another voluntary approach was subscription, a forerunner of current pledging systems. Church members would sign up on a publicly distributed list and agree to provide a certain amount of money or a specific quantity of in-kind gifts for use by the pastor and the ministry of the church. Methodists favored this practice, while Baptists rejected it. Some Presbyterian ministers refused to accept a call until they had reviewed the subscription list of the church.[24]

The sale and rental of pews was another approach to raising money for the church. This practice continued into the twentieth century, although there was a growing reaction against it. Meanwhile, voluntary offerings taken during the services were being used in some congregations for the support of the church, but were reserved for benevolent societies in many others. These offerings grew out of the intense missionary fervor that developed during the nineteenth century.[25]

The need for money to run church programs has created a certain awkwardness from the very beginning. Although the kingdom of God is to be built as an alternative to the kingdom of Mammon, some of the "filthy lucre" is necessary to fund the kingdom of God. Only in this century has the voluntary offering system become commonplace as a main source of church funding.

As we can see from the above chronology, there are certainly strong historical reasons to distrust the practice of tithing. However, since this discipline was endorsed by Jesus, it is time to recover our Christian heritage and not allow past mistakes to limit the work of the church in these critical times. In our period of economic success, we need to take a new approach to this old idea. Because tithing has been abused does not mean that we cannot reclaim it as a helpful guide. Given the fact that many of us are wealthier than our spiritual ancestors could have dreamed possible, some of us should even be able to exceed the tithe out of our love and enthusiasm for God.

We can rediscover the value of tithing in the statement by Irenaeus, writing in the second century. He affirmed that Jesus' teaching went even beyond the tithe and that the remarkable thing was that gifts are to be given "not as slaves but as freemen."[26] This comment hearkens back to the admonition in 1 Peter 2:16: "Live as free men, but do not use your freedom as a cover-up for evil; live as servants of God."

In a time when advertising competes so effectively for our dollars, the tithe can also serve as a helpful defense against media ploys. If we make up our minds that one-tenth of our income belongs to God right off the top, we save ourselves the agonizing monthly debates over how much to spend or keep for ourselves and how much to give. Setting aside a given percentage at the beginning of the week, as Paul advises in 1 Corinthians 16:2, will ensure that our offering is available.

Jacques Ellul, in his book *Money and Power*, suggests that giving money away is one of the surest ways to break its power over us. He notes that Jesus warned us that Mammon is actively competing with God for our souls, and that we have to make a choice. Our embarrassment over talking about money is one sign of how sacred we hold it. You can now bring up almost any topic in polite company, Ellul suggests, but when someone raises the issue of money the awkward silence that follows indicates that a social blunder has been made. We must "desacramentalize" money. Since the motivating force of money is to accumulate it, the spiritual counterforce is to give it away.[27]

The tithe is not only a practical solution to the difficult problem of knowing how much to keep and how much to give. It is an approach that can serve as a spiritual weapon against the forces that would steal our hearts and loyalties from Jesus Christ.

Is Money the Answer?

In this chapter on giving, we must finally look at another important question: Is money really the answer for the worldwide problems we are considering? Let it be stated that money is only part of the answer to the spiritual and physical needs faced by hundreds of millions of people around the globe. But it is definitely *one* part, and an important part.

Using 30 to 50 billion dollars to address the worst of the world's physical ills will only provide the financial wherewithal. James P. Grant, executive director of UNICEF, has suggested that the resource most needed to reduce childhood mortality is the political will or common desire to do so. His comment implies that it is not that we cannot end the poverty conditions facing so many children, but that we have not chosen to do so.

How—and why—does one decide to change this situation? Jesus offers a practical approach. He said that "where your treasure is, there your heart will be also" (Matt. 6:21). Notice the order of the words. Where we put our treasure is where we can look for our hearts. Based on this reasoning, we might well find that as we begin to invest in the lives of the needy by increasing donations to the international programs of our congregations, we will become increasingly involved in the situations faced by the people we are helping. Quite likely, as our interest grows, we will begin to apply the same sort of ingenuity to their problems that we apply to so many other aspects of our lives.

From another perspective, someone may ask how money is relevant to the global problem of overpopulation. How does money address that situation? For one thing, as noted earlier, all the children born into terrible poverty conditions do not die. Although many do survive, they are often permanently harmed, mentally and/or physically, by their deprivations. We have an obligation to help these weakest of our neighbors and to prevent their younger brothers and sisters from being similarly damaged.

Helping to alleviate worldwide poverty conditions can also make an indirect contribution to curbing overpopulation. Societies in which the childhood death rate is high also tend to have high birth rates. Parents in these cultures seem to view having children as a kind of social security, among other things. Having a lot of children fuels their hopes that one or two will grow up healthy and care for the parents in old age. It is interesting to note, then, that there is evidence that as the child mortality rate drops, the birth rate begins to drop even faster.[28] One might conclude that the poverty that causes children to die or be damaged in their early years may actually be encouraging overpopulation.

Money which has been carefully applied to date really has made a positive difference. For example, the global death rate of children under five years of age from poverty conditions has been almost halved over the past four decades. Also, the percent of the world's population which is literate has increased from 56 percent to 72 percent while life expectancy has increased from 46 years to 63 years during the same period. The improvement of these important "quality of life" factors cannot be taken for granted. However, they demonstrate that progress is possible if an intentional effort is made.

Another way that money can help is by providing support for those who are willing to go out from among us and serve directly. Currently, great personal sacrifice is required of those who go abroad to serve others. One counselor who specialized in helping missionaries recounted the tearful complaint of a couple who was serving overseas. They experienced guilt because their children had to suffer physical deprivation so the parents could be faithful to their calling. The writer tells of the wife's struggle with anger and bitterness. Although willing to sacrifice to preach the gospel, she challenged, "Who cares about us?"[29]

Indeed, one mission executive has said that the most difficult task his field personnel face is coming to terms with the incredible needs that confront them among the people they serve. "Most of our missionaries are surrounded by greater needs than we can give them resources to meet. This is one of the most difficult things for missionaries to resolve."[30]

If you are unable to throw your knapsack on a boat or backpack on a plane and head off for parts unknown, you still have a very important part to play in meeting world needs. The very career you are pursuing here at home is an important piece in the plan to share the Good News of Jesus Christ in word and deed. As support personnel, our giving allows us to play a role in the unfolding of God's story in the world.

Table 1

A Comparison of International Mission Support with American Lifestyle Expenditures

1. In 1987, U. S. Protestant agencies received $1.73 billion for overseas ministries.[31]

2. In 1985, Americans spent:
   a. $3.5 billion on cut flowers.[32]
   b. $8 billion on pets.[33]
   c. $2 billion on the lawn industry.[34]

3. In 1987, Americans spent:
   a. $3.5 billion on women's sheer hosiery.[35]
   b. $350 million on microwave popcorn.[36]
   c. $2.9 billion worth of quarters on video games and $2.6 billion worth of quarters on pinball machines.[37]

    d. approximately $1.7 billion of the $2.3 billion home video market on Nintendo games.[38]

    e. $2.7 billion on skin care.[39]

    f. $2 billion on golf equipment.[40]

    g. $2.5 billion on chewing gum.[41]

    h. $1.2 billion on wholesale sales of auto sound equipment.[42]

    i. $5 billion on new pools and accessories.[43]

4. In 1988, Americans spent:

    a. $12 billion on candy.[44]

    b. $29 billion on diets and diet-related products and services.[45]

    c. $35 billion on sports activities,[46] including:

        (1) $9.6 billion in sports-equipment sales that included:
        guns and hunting equipment, $1.9 billion;
        exercise equipment, $1.4 billion;
        sports clothing, $4.8 billion;
        sports shoes, $3.8 billion.[47]

        (2) $9.4 billion worth of boats, with two-thirds estimated to be for recreational use.[48]

5. In 1989, Americans spent:

    a. $44 billion on soft drinks.[49]

    b. $2.05 billion on movie tickets in the three months between Memorial Day and Labor Day.[50]

    c. $19.5 billion on state lottery tickets as part of the $246.9 billion legal gambling activity in the U.S.[51]

    d. $1.5 billion on the fingernail industry, including nail art.[52]

3
The Vision Unfolds

Developing a Global Strategy

*W*hatever happened to Poland? Or Nicaragua? Where have Panama, Ethiopia, and the Philippines gone?

Of course, geographically speaking, none of these countries has actually moved. From another point of view, however, after dominating the media for weeks at a time, all of these crisis-ridden countries gradually disappeared from the headlines, apart from an occasional mention. And with them went the public's awareness and understanding that their problems still existed.

The church's attention is just as easily diverted.

Facing Reality

One Sunday, in a congregation with which we are familiar, a special speaker used the sermon time to talk about her recent trip to the Philippines. At the beginning of her talk, people were sitting up attentively in their seats. The speaker's anger at the dismal living conditions she had seen in her overseas visit thundered over those in the pews. Shoulders gradually slumped as her listeners began to feel vaguely guilty about the conditions being brought to their attention. It was important to hear these things—what was to be done? The speaker returned to her own town.

The next Sunday, in the same church, a charming young missionary was visiting from a Central American country. He was funny and inspiring, obviously having committed his youth and energy to the lives of these people in desperate need. He worked closely with the local church there. The extent to which he identified with the people he served made him all the more appealing. As he shared personal stories, tears rolled down the cheeks of some of those in the pews, especially when he talked about the suffering of the children. When he concluded his sermon, there was an approving murmur among the listeners. Something must be done. He returned to the field.

Within weeks, another missionary came for a series of special seminars with the congregation. The congregation had regularly contributed support to her efforts in South America. She had several small group sessions during her visit, as well as the Sunday sermon. People were glad to hear of her work. The church felt good about supporting her. Something was being done.

A couple of weeks later, there was a special offering. For Bangladesh.

Four different regions of the world. All had desperate needs. This church was taking seriously its responsibility to challenge its members. Still, the congregation would have to work hard not to be discouraged by concluding that the world is really in terrible shape. These Christians—and others like them—all agree that *something* should be done about all of these situations. But, as our attention switches from one area of the world to another, it is easy to feel overwhelmed and helpless.

The word *overwhelmed* often comes up in workshops we conduct among church people. As we present facts about world needs, we ask people to consider one word that describes their response. Do you remember your own response to that exercise at the beginning of chapter 2? Compare your word to what we hear in workshops: "Shocked." "Desperate." "Discouraged." "Angry." "Overwhelmed."

There is little doubt that in many areas of the world, people are living in desperate conditions. From our work in congregations, we have concluded that people in churches across the United States really do care about these needs. Again and again, workshop participants, sometimes with tears in their eyes, confess their pain at not being able to relieve the misery of these distant neighbors. But what, they say with anguish, can we do?

We believe that something *can* be done. As demonstrated in chapter 2, people in this country are some of the richest in the history of the world. Even in the recession of the early 1990s, most of us are faced with merely forsaking a few luxuries temporarily, not being forced into the desperate living standards that much of the rest of the world endures. However, even in our affluence, we are giving a decreasing percentage of our income to our churches.

As we have more income, we also seem to have more "needs"—like in the story about the college student who was so touched by a tithing sermon that after the service he went up to the minister and made a commitment to give 10 percent of his income from that day forward. He immediately began to give out of his meager allowance; when he got his first job, he faithfully gave the church 10 percent of each paycheck he received.

Before long, this clever young man had designed a particular tool for the electronics industry, and his invention was purchased for a surprising sum. Now wealthy, he not only continued to tithe, but he invested wisely and began his own company. The business was such a great success that the tithe checks he wrote annually were more than the entire budget of the church he had attended in college. This disturbed him— was it sensible for him to be giving away that much money?

The man returned for a visit with the pastor of his college days. After the pastor congratulated him on his success, and they had exchanged other pleasantries, the once-struggling student got to the point: "Look, Pastor, I want you to let me out of this tithing arrangement. I'm giving ridiculous sums to the church. Even if I only gave 5 percent, I would be donating more money than most churches see in a year. How about it?"

The pastor looked at him kindly and said, "Well, I'll tell you, that agreement was not between you and me. It was really between you and God, so I am not in a position to make the changes you are asking for. But here's what I *can* do. I can pray for you, and ask God to decrease your income to the point where you feel comfortable tithing again."

Of course, ideally, this man should have realized that he was able to give much *more* than a tithe, once he had reached a basic living standard. But money has a strange effect on us. Once it is in our hands, it becomes "ours" in a very permanent way. As Jacques Ellul says, it almost seems to have a spiritual power; its insistence on being accumulated exerts a strong influence over our wills.[1] As we get more and more, we seem to have less and less to give away. In a related development, even as our society becomes richer, the influence of the church—the church that has been receiving a smaller portion of our incomes—appears to be declining. One Gallup poll found that people perceive the church to be losing influence in society.[2] A survey by the Barna Research Group reported a similar finding.[3] Juvenal, the Roman philosopher, recognized this tendency two millennia ago. He looked at Roman society and concluded that affluence is more destructive than war.[4]

It is not really surprising that world need is perceived as so overwhelming that people withdraw from the facts and become numb. In one sense, this may even be defined as a healthy coping mechanism; few people can daily face the idea of hopeless failure and maintain a sense of balance. However, we also need to understand the bad side effects of such withdrawal. As we increasingly turn our attention inward, we spend more and more money on ourselves. Because we then find less and less available for the work of the church, the church is limited in its ability to meet the world needs that so discourage us. We— and the rest of society—therefore conclude that the church is not offering any really effective strategy for coping with these conditions. The general perception is that the church is losing its influence on American culture.

For those of us who value democracy, that loss of positive impact should be a very real cause for concern. In the founding of this nation, the important place that religious values held was clearly recognized. "'Of all dispositions and habits which lead to political prosperity,' George Washington said in his farewell address, 'religion and morality are indispensable supports.'"[5] Yet, for all our progress and centuries of history, we are only seeing confirmed the proverbial wisdom—without a vision, the people perish.

Our wealth is a resource and an opportunity, but with no vision for its positive use, it can easily lead to licentiousness, overindulgence, excess. Should we feel bad about our present state of malaise? On the one hand, our preoccupation with material things is not surprising. After all, we are in an economic condition unique in the history of the world. The general affluence in our society is only about forty years old, a blip in the lifeline of history. It might take some time to gain perspective on the change in our condition.

On the other hand, it is time we "wake up and smell the coffee," as Ann Landers is so fond of saying. We have been like happy children in a candy store. This image is incomplete unless we recognize that children overeating on candy are only hurting themselves. While we have been gorging on symbolic chocolates and peppermints, those outside in the street have literally been wasting away, without even enough rice to fill their stomachs.

Let's continue with that metaphor a little farther. For years now we have "stuffed our faces" with all the good things we could grab, to the point of bursting. It has been fun in many ways. But we also have the "toothaches and stomach pains" to show for such behavior—there is a growing anxiety that society is in trouble. We need to realize that candy is still a treat, but that it must fit into the larger scheme of things. Maybe the wisdom of our elders is not so wrong, after all, and we are ready to mature a little. "Candy can ruin your appetite for dinner" no longer sounds like an empty slogan. We need solid food to grow spiritually, as Paul admonishes in 1 Corinthians 3:2.

It has taken time for us to recognize just how much abundance we have. If we are honest with ourselves, perhaps we can admit that we have not been all that eager to understand the responsibilities that come with this increased affluence. In any case, we must not stretch God's patience and mercy too far. God seems to have been tolerant of our overindulgence during the last few decades. But, with society fraying at the edges and the church losing its influence, we are risking his anger if we continue to close our hearts to our responsibilities.

We may have included "justice" as one of the items on our religious agenda, but too often as a lower priority and only because it was on the official list of the faith. Yet, if we are really Christians, we need to embrace this concept more fully, in all its true meaning. *Justice* means offering the opportunity for all people to hear how much God loves them through Jesus Christ.[6] *Justice* means sharing our resources so that parents need not helplessly watch their children die. *Justice* means loving our neighbors—near and far—at the same level of quality and care with which we love ourselves.

Justice is a strong theme of the Old Testament prophets. A recent reading through those books found this recurring refrain. Again and again, the prophets condemn the people's self-indulgence and lack of concern for others. Dire consequences are detailed and threatened with great authority. Warnings are issued. Then follows a remarkable conclusion: If people will change their ways, God will embrace them instead of punish them. One powerful example is in Isaiah 58:7–9:

> "Is it [true fasting] not to share your food with the hungry and to provide the poor wanderer with shelter—when you see the naked, to clothe him, and not to turn away from your own flesh and blood? Then your light will break forth like the dawn, and your healing will quickly appear; then your righteousness will go before you, and the glory of the LORD will be your rear guard. Then you will call, and the LORD will answer; you will cry for help, and he will say: Here I am."

Especially over the past forty years, many church members in North America, along with the rest of society, have become richer and richer. As we approach a new millennium, we should ask ourselves, "What are we going to do with the opportunities before us?"

The Need for a Plan

Our experience with church people indicates that there is an appetite to respond to needs across town and around the world. What seems to be missing is a clear agenda. Lacking a clear-cut strategy, people have been focusing their resources on themselves. To help us change those established patterns, we need to know in what direction we want to go. At this point, we will focus on the international problems. In chapter 5, we will consider a domestic strategy.

People care about world conditions but they have so much information about so many countries that they tend to be overwhelmed and to withdraw. The conclusion: Help concerned people have enough information about *one* place where they can make a difference.

At first blush, this idea seems to recommend itself strongly because it seems so logical. If we can't understand everything everywhere, maybe we can understand something somewhere. If we can't keep track of Nicaragua and Bangladesh and Mozambique and Laos, maybe we should try to learn about one country in depth. Perhaps, by becoming specialists about conditions facing people in one area of the world, we could learn some basic truths that will help us understand general conditions in many other areas of the world. If we can begin to realize what our gifts can and do accomplish in one place, we might be encouraged to increase our giving to make an even greater impact there. One pastor, who had a history of deep concern about people in need around the globe, shared out of a sense of desperation, "Do you mean I could kind of forget about everyplace else and actually succeed *someplace?*"

In this context, it might be helpful to reflect on some sound business principles. It is a common axiom in business that one needs clearly defined goals and specific strategies to approach success. Planning is a key element in having any hope of making a dent in the marketplace. Without long- and short-term goals, there is no sense of direction, and the company cannot know when or if success has been attained.

Let us state emphatically what you are probably already thinking: The church is *not* a business! We know that. The church is the earthly manifestation of Christ's body, through which the Holy Spirit should be able to work to accomplish God's purpose for the world. You have no argument from us on this point, but now let's look at one of Jesus' more intriguing comments, found in the parable of the shrewd manager (Luke 16:1–9). Commenting on that wicked servant (who failed in his task and then gave discounts to his master's debtors so they would welcome him when he was out of a job), Jesus notes that "the people of this world are more shrewd in dealing with their own kind than are the people of the light" (v. 8). It would seem that if we are really interested in coming out of our shells and bringing light to our neighbors, we can learn from a variety of sources.

Consider the comment of a successful businessman who is also a lay leader in his church. He had asked us to do an analysis of denominational financial patterns in terms of mission support. We found that mission expenditures of his denomination had gone down. This trend was accompanied by another strong pattern: The congregations had been allocating a smaller and smaller portion of their budgets to denominational programs. In fact, a decreasing portion of their total budgets had been going out of the congregations for any reason. These congregations had been gradually keeping a greater portion of their total budgets for themselves.

In his response to our report, the businessman wrote with real anguish, "If we ran our own businesses the way we run the Lord's business, we'd all be bankrupt."

Although the church is not a business in the usual sense of the word, that is no excuse for poor performance. Precisely because we are most directly conducting the *Lord's* business through our churches, we should be even better and more creative managers than we are in our private activities. Therefore, we have concluded that it is defensible to explore a strategy to help church members in the United States specialize in one area of the world. Learning to care more deeply about the people there may be a creative way to motivate Christians to spend less on themselves and direct more of their resources to help others.

But What About . . . ?

Before considering what our strategy might look like, responding to a few common objections to the general notion we have proposed will clarify what we are talking about.

"We don't want to return to 'comity.'" The idea of congregations specializing in one area of the world sets off alarm bells for some people who are familiar with church history. At the turn of the last century, there was a strategy called *comity.* This meant that certain European countries, and later the United States, divided up the world into spheres of influence. Remember the *Belgian* Congo? *French* Equatorial Africa? India was a British "colony" until the 1940s. And for many years Germany, England, and the United States each had provinces in China that they basically controlled. This dividing up of the globe meant that a First World power dominated business and politics in its satellite country. It also meant that missionaries from the controlling country felt a particular responsibility for the people in that area.

Today, comity has been discredited, largely because there was no partnership between the two countries involved. Instead, one country, more powerful because of its military strength, brought the other under painful submission. Respect for the history and traditions of the occupied area rarely existed. Even church representatives were sometimes seen as forcing their ways upon others. In China, for example, a popular observation is that "guns came down one plank of the ship and missionaries came down the other." In Guangzhou, a city in southern China formerly called Canton, the guidebooks still refer to the sign at the bridge to an island where foreigners, including many missionaries, lived. It read, "No Chinese or dogs allowed."

No, the time is past for such lopsided relationships. If we can learn anything from this painful history, it is that sharing our faith with others must be done out of servanthood, not the desire to impose our views through use of power. When God took on flesh and entered history, he did not arrive with legions of angels to read humans the riot act (although Revelation promises that, in his absolute sovereignty, he has not permanently ruled out this strategy). God came to us as the embodiment of loving service. We should do no less.

But, even though this area-to-area division as it developed through comity was abused, there is no reason to reject the basic concept. While matching areas was imposed and not voluntary in the past, the idea of establishing area-to-area relationships does offer some inherent strengths. Because we are intelligent creatures, through God's grace we can learn not to repeat our mistakes as we move forward in creative ways.

"Our congregation is already committed to specific mission efforts." In any given congregation, there are bound to be several wide-flung mission commitments already in existence. Whenever the idea of specialization comes up, you can feel the hackles rise among those with vested interest in these historical ties. One might hear comments like, "We've supported this

mission since the church sent out So-and-so twenty years ago."
Or "We had a special speaker who moved us so deeply that we
immediately made a five-year pledge." Or "This region of our
denomination has accepted a 'second-mile' giving relationship
with our churches in X country, and that doesn't fit with a general area-to-area strategy that includes other denominations."

The concept of the area-to-area strategy that we are dis-
cussing need not disturb any of these current commitments.
Remember, we are talking about the challenge of *increasing*
mission support. All the current activities in your congregation
are probably being funded with a relatively low level of per-
member giving, and even that low level may be dropping. The
area-to-area approach is not designed to replace current commitments. Keep them all! In fact, it is possible that church
members who grow in sophistication and understanding of one
area of the world might even want to strengthen their understanding of, and commitment to, the current efforts in other
areas.

An area-to-area strategy is meant to encourage giving *over
and above current levels.* If average per-member giving is less
than 2.5 percent of income and declining, this new approach
will target funds that would be contributed *above* this percentage. Those resources are not now coming into the church.
Thus, there should be enough money for current commitments
as well as for additional ones.

If geographical focusing becomes generally accepted by our
churches, your congregation might not be matched with any
area of the world where you now support mission work. And
Christians in some other part of the United States will probably
be matched with countries of your congregation's current concern. But, in the same way that you will be acquiring a deeper
understanding of one country, those church members will be
learning about one of the countries to which you are currently

committed. If they become *really* interested in the people of that country, they will increase their giving—which will be added to your ongoing support of the work there. Ultimately, the mission work in any one area can actually be expanded.

On the other hand, suppose we do not use an area-to-area strategy, and each congregation continues to support mission efforts through the present patchwork system. Congregation members will lack any clear approach for meeting world needs. If past patterns continue, they will withdraw more and more from mission involvement. Their giving will continue to decline, meaning there will be less available for mission support. Although your church may maintain its traditional ties to certain mission activities, in the long run it is probable that the mission work you value will suffer funding shortfalls.

The fact that change is often perceived as loss has become a conventional axiom. Yet, if we really care about those in need around the world, we must allow our traditions to be threatened a little bit. As we seek to love God with our minds and our hearts (Matt. 22:37), we need to open ourselves to the task at hand. When logic dictates changing the way we have traditionally chosen our mission focus, we should be open to the idea that such a change might actually be the best route to take.

"Our denomination does not have a work in the area with which we are matched." This apparent problem has an exciting solution. We have been told that, at the national level, there is a great deal of cooperation between denominational offices in terms of mission work. Groups that have a resource in a particular country are often willing to share it with others. Importing items, providing transportation or medical care, and other important aspects of overseas ministry are often conducted on an interdenominational basis or through groups that do not represent a specific denomination. In fact, denomina-

tional differences are often emphasized more strongly at home than they are in other countries.

We can learn a lot about cooperation from our brothers and sisters who are serving in other countries. We can support our denominational offices as they work in tandem with a sister denomination that has an existing work in the area with which we are matched. Likewise, members of another denomination may begin supporting our own established works in a given country.

Some cooperative agencies are already in place. These organizations, such as World Relief of the National Association of Evangelicals or Church World Service of the National Council of the Churches of Christ in the U.S.A., can serve as our representatives. They may also have the important role of "brokering" between denominations, channeling resources from the churches in one part of the United States in a particular denomination to a like-minded denomination's work in the area of the world with which they are matched.

The fact that few, if any, denominations have mission work in every country in the world need not be a problem. This very weakness may well be a reason to strengthen the body of Christ. The church is that body, as Paul writes in 1 Corinthians 12. Each part needs the other. Unfortunately, while there is practical cooperation on the actual mission field, there is insufficient coordination between denominations in relating to the global task that mutually confronts them.

We have a good friend who has cerebral palsy, a condition that affects muscle coordination. Although our friend's brain might signal his arm to go from right to left, his body will not respond correctly. It also takes great concentration for him to put one foot in front of the other to climb a set of stairs, because his rebellious leg insists on going in the wrong direction. The three of us worked together on projects that encourage oneness in the body of Christ and we would sometimes be exasperated at the unwillingness of Christians to cooperate with each other. We once all laughed in the midst of our frustration as we reflected that, rather than functioning as an athlete running a race with purpose, the body of Christ often acts as if it had cerebral palsy. From this lovely brother's weakness, we have been able to gain insight that may help us strengthen the church's functioning as a united body.

Will we continue to be divided as Christians, building walls between each other and maintaining our own spheres of influence? If we recognize that there are people overseas who are stating a willingness to work with us to make an impact on so many desperate conditions, we will be open to new ways of working together. And we might find these new ways have positive consequences for all of us.

A final word on this point: We are not suggesting that any congregation or denomination give up its identity and meld into some kind of generic blob. There are strengths in our differences. Some people like formal services; some like spontaneity. Some like three-hour worship times; others set their alarms for one hour after the prelude begins. If we are truly one body, we don't want all eyes or all fingers. We should be able to combine those differences in some sort of creative arrangement wherein we strengthen and support each other in pursuing God's purposes.

Advantages of an Area-to-Area Approach

There are many practical advantages to having Christians in the United States approach world needs in a more specialized fashion. We have already mentioned that such a focus would allow each individual to screen out much of the overly abundant information about many different parts of the world and keep ears and heart open to learning about one area in-depth. However, there are six other considerations that strengthen the appeal of this idea.

1. *Avoiding Duplication.* Presently, there is little coordination in the allocation of Christian agency efforts in global missions. As a result, duplication is not uncommon, and scarce mission resources are not distributed around the globe as judiciously as they could be. An analysis of United States Protestant mission agencies is informative on this point. Consider that Europe, with its strong Christian tradition, has 10.5 percent of the world's population but is assigned almost 16 percent of mission agencies' focus. Oceania has 0.56 percent of the world's population, and somewhat over 4 percent of agency focus. Latin America, with 9 percent of the world's population, is earmarked for 33 percent of mission agency activity.

On the other hand, Africa, with 12.5 percent of the globe's population, but with serious physical concerns, has 20 percent of the Protestant mission agency activity from this country. And Asia—which has 62 percent of the world's population—has attracted only a quarter of the mission agency activity and personnel.

Of course, some of the agency activity in, for example, Europe is focused on groups that are accessible in Europe but not in their own "closed" countries.

And the level of need in Africa or Latin America certainly justifies involvement by concerned Christians from abroad.

Meanwhile, many Asian countries have not been receptive to mission workers from abroad, which would naturally limit the number of agencies that could be involved there. However, many Asian countries are opening up, and the possibility of real partner relationships is developing as world dynamics change.

International politics do not fully explain the present skewed circumstances of mission activity. For example, Ralph Winter of the U.S. Center for World Mission asserts that 90 percent of Protestant missionaries are working in areas where the church has already been planted. Although he affirms that these people are doing a tremendous job, he comments, "Where the church has not been planted, nothing happens!"[7]

Unfortunately, mission activities are often underrepresented in areas of the world that are suffering the greatest physical need. A 1987 World Food Council report notes this disparity: "Hunger was growing in Asia, Africa and Latin America. While public attention has recently been focused on Africa because of the natural disasters there, the fact remained that today some 60 percent of the hungry live in Asia, against 25 percent in Africa, 10 percent in Latin America and 5 percent in the Middle East."[8] In fact, of the 38,000 children under age five who die daily from poverty conditions, 40 percent are in three Asian countries: India, Pakistan and Bangladesh.[9]

It would seem that a patchwork approach to mission focus does not reflect a sensible sharing of Christian concern. Certain areas of the world are in desperate need and yet receive limited attention, while other areas are rich in mission resources.

2. Longevity of Support. There is another advantage to moving away from a situation where public support is generated by the media, rather than by a church-initiated strategy. Currently, even mission efforts in countries receiving a lot of aid cannot necessarily count on unflagging concern and regular assistance. If congregations were matched with particular areas, the support for mission projects would be more ongoing.

You might remember from chapter 1 how our hearts were seared when we talked with Diether Jäckel, director of the agency in Brazil. We had seen heart-rending conditions in Northeast Brazil, and at the end of our trip he was talking quite freely with us. Diaconia's superintendent seemed most sincere when he indicated that he really did hope that Africa would receive the aid it needed, especially if another drought and related famine developed there. But he was also very clear that if media attention shifted from the serious drought in Brazil to one in Africa, the works in Brazil would suffer. A major concern he had was that there would be no funds for development work, for activities that might alleviate some of the conditions imposed by the cyclical droughts in Brazil. There can be no long-term solutions if aid comes and goes in a more irregular pattern than the natural disasters. Instead, agencies that should be working to solve the underlying problems are forced into handling only emergencies. If Christians in one area of the United States were committed to helping the area in which Jäckel worked, regardless of whether or not there was an immediate crisis, Diaconia could begin to make some inroads into limiting the destructive effects of the cycle of natural disasters.

A more recent analogy to this situation has to do with Bible distribution. We were talking with an official of a Bible society soon after the remarkable change in attitude by the former U.S.S.R. toward the importation of Bibles. Although this official was delighted at the positive response from Christians in the United States to this opportunity to send Bibles to a formerly closed country, he did have one deep concern. He noted that supporters, on the whole, were not making *larger* contributions. Rather, they were merely redirecting their present support of ongoing efforts to this new initiative. He was happy to have funds for the U.S.S.R. project, but meanwhile there were expenses for ongoing Bible distribution in other parts of the world to be met. That's usually what happens with media-driven funding. The pie doesn't necessarily get bigger; the total amount of resources is just shared in a different way. Sometimes the slices are smaller for everyone.

In any case, church workers in desperate areas of need around the world generally face such a scarcity of resources for the important work of changing the root causes of local problems that they are often limited to meeting crises only. That is but one reason why it is important to think about increasing the size of the pie and maintaining continuity in the help being given to a particular area. Mission efforts need to get beyond crisis-management into long-term sharing.

3. *End-Use Information.* While some congregation members may express a willingness to direct more of their resources to mission work, there is generally one reservation: "I want to be sure the money will do some good." For example, an older gentleman who participated in one of our workshops was a faithful church attender, a businessman, and a lay leader. He was concerned about an imminent famine in Ethiopia, the second for that decade. We were in open discussion when he said, with visible pain on his face, "I want to help this time. But nobody told me what my gifts did last time."

When we talk about increasing our mission giving, there is generally at least one person who will ask us, "How do I know my denomination will make good use of the money?" Our answer always is, "You will have to ask *them.*" What we mean is that contributors need to maintain a dialogue with their denominational office, an all-too-rare occurrence.

Our encounters with denominational representatives lead us to conclude that they are committed individuals who have a wealth of information. Many denominations have individuals with great expertise in specific areas of the world who are delighted for the opportunity to visit at the congregational level and share their treasure trove of information with interested people. However, we have been told that—under the present system—few congregations extend invitations to these resource people, simply because there is not much reason to learn about one particular area of the world.

This distancing between denominational offices and congregations apparently had its historical roots in the mid-1920s. After World War I, benevolences for missions began to increase rapidly. Church members were learning about world conditions through visits of missionaries to their congregations and were responding generously. Activity reached such a height that pastors began to complain to their denominational headquarters that they could not educate the congregation about global concerns (and entertain the missionaries needed to do so) and still fulfill their regular pastoral duties.

The solution at the denominational level was to institute stewardship boards that were to control the interpretation of mission activity. As a result, fewer missionaries came to the congregations, and fund-raising efforts were generalized—allocated to a "unified budget," which included missions. By 1929, benevolence giving had visibly dropped.[10]

Of course, it would not be a creative solution if an area-to-area strategy were to force pastors to take on the role of mission educator and add that task to his or her already-busy schedule. Yet, the distance that has developed between the mission agencies and congregations in some denominations seems to limit the willingness of church members to give. Although mission work in many denominations is now underfunded, we believe that an area-to-area strategy can help change this situation. The mission committee of a congregation could become familiar with the denominational staff responsible for the area of the world with which the congregation is matched. Returning missionaries would not be marketed from Maine to California, but would educate a ready-made audience in a general geographical area of the United States. Denominational policies in the matched area of the world could be explored and understood by the congregations involved in the work there.

There might be some people who will suggest that denominational leaders will groan at the extra work such an arrangement would require. Such officials (surely a minority!) might complain that people at the congregational level often ask basic questions that should not have to be answered again and again. It is generally easier to move faster if the resources are just made available, without having to explain and justify every policy to contributors. And it is quite possible that people at the congregational level lack all the information necessary to understand some of the sophisticated sensitivities needed to undertake effective mission work.

A few denominational officials may indeed see this area-to-area approach as an additional drain on their time and energy. However, with mission support declining, some way to encourage increased giving at the congregational level must be found. If congregation-level education will initially require extra work, it is because such efforts will be making up for lost time. Church members cannot be asked to increase their giving—to deny themselves and their children certain luxuries and "nicer" necessities—if they do not share a sense of mutuality of purpose with their denominational officials.

If congregation members ask "basic questions," those basic questions really do need to be answered. An acquaintance of ours remembers a high-school chemistry teacher who knew his subject backwards and forwards and was doing some important research in the field. Our friend, however, had a greater bent toward the liberal arts. She was willing to try to learn chemistry, but it took a great deal of mental effort on her part. She eventually got an *A* in the course, but she still reflects the anger she felt about being treated by the teacher as if she were "stupid." This student learned chemistry to prove him wrong, though some of the basic concepts and definitions were confusing to her at the start. She learned, but it would have been easier if the teacher had been her partner in the effort, rather than her adversary.

To the extent that a denomination feels the need for greater cooperation at the local level, its leaders must trust their congregational supporters with enough information so that church members can be full partners in the work. In the same way, the members must learn to increase their trust in their denominational representatives, respecting their experience and accumulated wisdom. The end result could well be a powerful engine for social justice and for proclaiming the gospel of Jesus Christ in both word and deed.

In any case, because an area-to-area strategy would allow congregations to ask their denominations for ongoing end-use information about how their support was being used, they would learn what a difference their gifts were making possible.

4. *Self-Education Efforts.* An area-to-area strategy would also motivate people in a congregation to see their international partners' efforts firsthand. For example, if you wanted to use your vacation time to visit a mission field, would you know where to go? You would probably have several choices available to you, yet one would not recommend itself more strongly than another. But, with an area-to-area focus, travel goals could be directed toward the country of specialization. A few brave souls would make the first trek, and when they return enthusiastically—as people who visit mission work overseas invariably do—they can encourage others to go. A routine of visiting, and perhaps even exchanges, can be started.

On the local level, people could make a point of reaching out to international guests from their matched area. For example, many international students are very interested in getting to know Americans, but the existing channels are often underutilized. Local residents are usually not as interested in meeting foreign students as these students are interested in befriending North Americans. While reaching out to international visitors in general is to be recommended, an area-to-area approach to mission activity gives us an added incentive to get to know students from a particular country.

5. *Personalized Concern.* Another reason an area-to-area strategy recommends itself is that this kind of specialization encourages personalized concern. A variation on the idea of area-to-area matching is the "adopt-a-child" projects that are routinely successful for mission agencies. One denominational official noted that people who "adopt" a child overseas tend to be more generous over a longer period of time than those who merely contribute to general development activities or even to a particular crisis.

The same personalization associated with sponsoring a child can be encouraged between individuals in a congregation and people in the overseas area with which they are linked. Getting to know the customs and traditions of the people in one country of the world increases interest in that region. We've seen this to be true in the case of friends of ours. They have two sons. When they were still little, the two brothers could go to the world map and find both Northeast Brazil, because that's where Champaign County churches were sending help, and China, because a foreign scholar they had met lived there. The rest of the countries may have appeared to be a blur to their young eyes, but those countries stood out.

6. *Partners Instead of Providers.* Perhaps the best argument for an area-to-area strategy rests on the fact that a sense of friendship develops between two sets of people in this sort of context. As noted before, the idea of the "haves" controlling the "have-nots," such as existed in a comity relationship, has been thoroughly discredited. The present goal in any type of devel-

opment work is to encourage true partnering between those on both sides of the relationship.

People at the congregational level rarely have this opportunity today. It is true that some denominations have developed the option of designating second-mile giving projects, and these are certainly a step in the right direction. However, since these designations vary from congregation to congregation, even in the same town, no general understanding can develop among churches in one area of the United States about the reality of life in another part of the world. Furthermore, such commitments are vulnerable to the changing interests of the congregation. While one congregational leader may have fostered a particular interest in a certain Latin American country, if that person moves or retires, the next person to gain influence in the congregation may encourage shifting to a particular South Pacific project.

What all this means is that people at the congregational level are often forced into being providers only, as if money were the only need. On the other hand, at the denominational level, officials responsible for a particular area of the world soon develop contacts and friendships in other countries that provide them with a great deal of enthusiasm for doing a good job. Although an official may visit a congregation to tell of some of the terrific individuals he or she has met, it remains a distant, secondhand experience for the parishioners, touched though they may be.

However, an area-to-area strategy provides the potential for true partnership. The church member at home can ask questions and actually learn from the answers. Remember our embarrassing experience in Brazil in chapter 1? Unintentionally, we were trying to tell the director of Diaconia what he should do. When he wrote those important words—TRUST and RISK—on his pad of paper, we read them upside down and let them sink in. He never said a word to us about what the words implied, but that one encounter changed us from providers to partners in his work.

While many church members in the United States have more money than they know how to use constructively, millions of people in other countries (and locally, as we will touch on in chapter 5) desperately need our help. As strange as it may seem, their willingness to accept our excess actually helps us out of the decaying situation we now face due to our over-abundance—by giving us a positive agenda of discipleship to pursue. And the wisdom they have accumulated, less tainted by a preoccupation with materialism, may be very important for us to hear as we try to develop new identities, apart from how much we possess. However, the awkwardness of money will keep us at a distance from each other unless we can communicate our mutuality of interest. Then we all become partners and friends across the miles and cultures that now separate us. An area-to-area strategy is the most creative way to provide the opportunity for developing meaningful partnerships, to the benefit of all concerned.

A Yoking Map™

After going through the thought process described above, we were even more convinced that establishing long-term relationships between areas is of great importance in mission objectives. There was also no question in our minds that the resources exist among Christians in the United States to make such relationships truly beneficial abroad and meaningful at home. Although world need is great, the resources available to us are even greater. Just $2.5 billion a year, as much as Americans spend on chewing gum, could prevent many children's deaths and most of their malnutrition.[11] If the best estimate is that $30 to $50 billion a year can limit the worst of world poverty, it is no small matter that church members in the United States could provide that much and more, if giving were to increase to an average of 10 percent, *and the new funds were carefully earmarked to address these needs.*

But what is the logical and most practical way to distribute these resources? In the early 1980s, we set about the important task of adding enough substance to our idea that it would appear to be a viable option for interested Christians. The planning process we went through was an education in and of itself . . .

Defining Needs. Deciding what we meant by "need" was the first important step. In a world of such economic, political, and cultural diversity, how could one come up with a summary definition? As Christians, though sensitive to the necessity of meeting the body's physical requirements, we must also recognize that the spirit is an important component of human existence. It was somewhat surprising to find that definitions of even physical needs varied from source to source, and a clear consensus was not immediately available. Not to be discouraged, we forged a working definition that we felt to be defensible. "Need," for the purposes of developing the Yoking Map, was defined with both a physical and spiritual component. A country was defined as being in need if it met one or both of the following criteria:

It had less than the world's average per-capita gross national product (GNP).

It had less than 50 percent self-proclaimed Christians, according to *The World Christian Encyclopedia.*[12]

Those knowledgeable in measuring a country's wealth will rightly point out the limitations of using the per-capita gross national product as a determinant of physical need. The biggest problem is that GNP is merely a statistic that indicates the total market value of all the goods and services produced by a nation during a specified period of time. What the GNP does not indicate is how well the assets and income are *actually* distributed among the people. This is a serious concern. In many countries, those with more than enough are a small minority, while the vast majority of the population lives in desperate need. Thus, in a country with a respectable per-capita GNP, many of its citizens may be living in abject poverty.

However, the advantage of using the GNP is that it is available for every country. Also, it does not discriminate against those poor countries that are doing a good job in assisting their citizens to meet their basic needs. Here is an example. Although some systems, such as the Physical Quality of Life Index[13] or the Measurement of Human Suffering Index[14] include other important factors, such as literacy and infant mortality rates, consider Sri Lanka. It rated quite high on the PQLI because of some effective internal policies, but its per-capita GNP placed it in one of the neediest categories of the world's nations. If we had considered this country as not being in very great need, because the government had been faithful with what little it had (and therefore its PQLI was higher than certain other countries), we might actually have encouraged Sri Lanka to become less responsible in distributing its available resources so as to qualify for more assistance from abroad! Using per-capita GNP, while not ideal, at least gave us a general basis for comparison.

In terms of spiritual need, we opted to base our definition of "self-proclaimed Christians" on *The World Christian Encyclopedia.* Again, standards used to count unreached peoples can vary greatly among agencies and denominations. However, David Barrett's comprehensive editing of this reference work gave a standard of comparison for the world's nations.

Because of the extra expense of meeting physical needs, the per-capita GNP factor was weighted ten-to-one with the evangelization factor.

Defining Available Resources. Calculating the funding potential that existed among Christians in the United States was a little easier. County-by-county figures for membership in historically Christian churches were available, as was per-capita income for all residents. If "average giving" was defined at 2.5 percent of income for that portion of the county population who were church members, the amount of current giving could be calculated. Then it was possible to calculate the difference between current giving and the potential amount at an average level of 10 percent giving. The major portion of the resulting figure was defined as being "available" for international mission work, constituting resources that could be applied to countries defined as being "in need."

Designing a Yoking Map. Using a mapping process, the theoretically "available" resources were distributed on an area-to-area basis to 145 countries, taking into account their degree of "need," as we had defined it. The results surprised us in many ways. A copy of the resulting Yoking Map is on pp. 148–49.

We began by "yoking" areas in Latin America to counties in Texas because of the shared heritage that resulted from their geographical proximity. We actually hoped that the Latin American countries could also be matched with states as far north as Illinois, so we could maintain Champaign County's continuing focus on Northeast Brazil. Instead, Latin America was fully matched by the time we were two-thirds into the state of Texas!

We then focused on the West Coast. Our first matching was between Alaska and the former U.S.S.R.—again because of the geographical closeness. We also felt that there was a cultural link between the Pacific Rim and the countries of Southeast Asia. As we matched, including Hawaii with Oceania, we were soon through the Southeast Asian region. When we began linking areas of the People's Republic of China with church members here, several state lines were crossed. Since the United States is sparsely settled in some of the larger western states, Christians in those states were soon matched with China. Continuing eastward, as the Midwest states through Ohio were also needed to complete this matching, we found ourselves amazed. The reality of just how populous that country is—and how limited is the presence of Christianity there—was staggering.

India and Central Asia were matched with Christians in our southeastern states, and Africa and the Middle East with our populous Northeast.

The Yoking Map literally astounded us! Although Latin America and Africa were highest in our own mission consciousness, our matching process had paired church members in fully two-thirds of the United States with *Asian* countries. Actually, we should have not been so surprised, since what we saw in this exercise merely reflected the finding of the World Food Council quoted previously. That is, in actual numbers, over half of the hungry people live in Asia. The fact that the church has not been firmly established in Asia was also well known.

Even so, the Yoking Map seemed strange, especially to one of us. Sylvia remembers her personal reaction to our first drafting of the map in 1984:

> I have to confess I was disappointed at the results. I had no interest in China at all. Also, I remember completing this matching and praying, "Lord, this really seems like a dumb idea. China has been closed to the West for much of the past

four thousand years, including up to the present. Here we are, sitting in the middle of the Midwest of the United States, with no possibility of meeting anyone from China. Are you sure this is a good plan?"

Nevertheless, we adopted the plan, and began to promote it through our work.

Unexpected Encouragement

By the spring of 1984, we were trying to publicize the idea of the Yoking Map in conjunction with our research on the potential of church giving to help meet world needs. But how were we going to encourage church members in over twenty states to develop a special interest in China? Mission agencies were still locked out of that country, even though our government was making progress in normalizing relations with China, which had withdrawn from international contacts during the Cultural Revolution. At this point, we were recommending the Yoking Map idea to others on the basis of faith alone, at least as it applied to China. Of course, the whole point of the journey of faith is that you step out in trust, even though not sure of where the next bend in the road might lead.

In June of 1984, we received a phone call at our office. A University of Illinois economics professor wondered if we could be of assistance to him. He was working with a visiting professor who had a most unusual request: She wanted to meet some poor people. We assured him that we would be happy to cooperate. Such introductions would not present any difficulty because, through our local works, we had developed friendships with people we could comfortably approach.

Well, the local professor went on, this visitor didn't just want to *meet* poor people, she wanted to live with them for a few days. Although this request was even more unusual, it interested us a great deal. We were spending our time encouraging Christians in the local community to get out and meet those in need personally. Here was someone who was asking us not only to introduce her, but also to arrange for her to live in the homes of one or two families. She obviously wanted to go the extra mile. We were not only willing to approach our friends with her request, we were eager to meet this person, whoever she was.

Well, said the local professor, there was one more detail that we really ought to know: The visitor's English wasn't all that good, which might make communication difficult.

Hmmm. This factor might mean the complication of arranging for a translator, which would take more time in our busy schedule. Where, we asked, was this professor from?

She was an economics professor from Peking University in the People's Republic of China!

The implications of that news struck like a thunderbolt. Here we had been doubting the practicality of the Yoking Map because we had no way to establish contacts in China. And now a professor from China was knocking at our door, asking to meet us. Was that celestial chuckling we heard?

The visiting professor was charming. Although her English was limited, she had one of those outgoing personalities that allowed her to communicate with a limited number of words. We easily arranged for her visits with two friends we knew—a family on public assistance with three generations living in the same house, and an elderly lady living alone on Social Security. We also hit it off so well personally that we spent enough time together to become friends.

Our new friend from the East invited us to a meeting of Chinese students on the university campus. The first Chinese students had arrived here in the early 1980s. By 1984, there were several hundred at the University of Illinois. We went, expecting an evening of "political education" in Chinese. Although we did see many standard blue Mao jackets, instead of lectures there were three movies scheduled. The first was in Chinese, about a blind student who overcomes his difficulties. The second was *The Way We Were,* with Barbara Streisand and Robert Redford, apparently selected by the leadership because it dealt with a social activist. We did not wait for *David Copperfield,* although many students stayed late into the night in the festival-like atmosphere.

The Chinese professor introduced us to several other professors and students from her country. We were so hungry for information about China that we took every available opportunity to talk with them.

Then, in 1985, three important things happened.

First, the visiting professor returned to China. This was a sad parting, because we had become very close. As we stood in the airport, it was with a feeling of deep regret that we would probably never see her again. Although we had always been clear that we were active and committed Christians, she had not seen this as a problem. Because of our work with local people in need, our commitment to Christ was not distancing in her mind, and we had had several talks, sharing our different perspectives on world conditions.

Our new friend refused to believe we would not soon be in touch. "You must come to China!" she had said many times. We would protest that we were too poor to travel, that we did not have money to take vacations in our own country, let alone internationally. She promised to get us teaching positions at her university. We could not go, we insisted. As founders and directing staff for a Christian research and service organization, we could not take time off, even though it would be important for our work for us to learn about China firsthand. She was not easily dissuaded. Only later did we find out that it is a distinction of Chinese culture that one must actively refuse several times before a gift or offer may be accepted!

The second significant development in 1985 was the founding of the Amity Foundation in China. The following quote describes the work of this organization:

> The Amity Foundation was created on the initiative of Chinese Christians for the purpose of promoting health, education, social service and rural development projects in the People's Republic of China. It is an independent Chinese voluntary organization which has received the support and encouragement of friends in China and overseas. Formally established in 1985, the Amity Foundation represents a new form of Christian involvement in Chinese society.[15]

As its literature states quite plainly, this is not a church organization. A key factor in the permission for the church in China to become active again—after its property had been confiscated and destroyed during the years of the Cultural Revolution and religious activity prohibited—was that the church remain a distinctly Chinese institution, "self-supporting, self-governing and self-propagating" (the Three Selfs). Therefore, contributions to the Amity Foundation "will not go toward the work of evangelism and church building of Chinese Christians."[16]

The chief significance of the Amity Foundation was that it was a mechanism whereby Christians in the West could reestablish partner relationships with Christians in China. Through this organization, funds could be accepted by Christians in China from Christians in the West and be applied to joint social-welfare projects. The barrier to international Christian cooperation that had effectively existed since the People's Republic of China was founded in 1949 had been removed, and new links could begin to be carefully crafted. Suddenly the possibility of Christians in over twenty states developing a special interest in the work of the church in China no longer seemed unrealistic.

The Invitation

The third significant development in 1985 was a telephone call we received late one night. The caller identified himself as a newly arrived graduate student from Beijing. His professor at Peking University wanted to know why we had not responded to her letter. His professor, of course, was our own friend, now teaching again in Beijing. Not having received the letter was our reason. Well, the caller went on, the university officials needed to know if we were coming to teach in China.

What? We had never said we were doing any such thing! Even so, it seemed that our professor friend had arranged for both of us to come and teach English, and the university officials needed to know if we were going to accept their invitation.

We were still stunned when we went to the office the next day and shared the news at a senior staff meeting. The two other staff present could not have been more supportive. "This is God moving," said one. "We'll do whatever is necessary," said the other. Both said, "You *must* go."

It was true that we had been working to promote the Yoking Map as a logical approach to mission concern and that twenty-two states were matched with the People's Republic of China, a country about which little was now known. It was also clear that other trusted people were confirming the value of the trip. Not only did the staff agree to take on our responsibilities during our absence, but the larger Christian community was extremely supportive. The trip was seen as a kind of sabbatical.

For fourteen years, we had accepted a very low salary, had lived in public housing for five years to build bridges with the local poor, and had worked to facilitate the involvement of church members with those in need. We were told it was time for a change of scenery. One congregation voted a special financial gift to help finance our travels, while others expressed a willingness to support the staff who would carry on the general work of *empty tomb* in any way they could. All these things seemed like confirmations that we ought to respond positively to the invitation.

Even so, while John felt moved to go, Sylvia had some doubts. Once again, she relates her feelings:

> I remember that the thought of China was deeply scary. It meant being away from family, and, as perhaps insignificant as it seems, I had never *not* been home on Christmas, the only day of the year my whole family gathers. I did not want to kick against the pricks of God's will. Still, it seemed too overwhelming to pick up and move to a foreign country, especially a country as very foreign as China was. Therefore, as I drafted the official application required, once we indicated a general willingness to go, I made our credentials sound as Christian as possible, thinking this would discourage the university from accepting us as teachers. I emphasized our work with churches in the United States and our task of involving them with the poor.

Even being so up-front about our Christian commitment did not result in the rejection of our applications. On the contrary, later on it appeared that our forthrightness actually seemed to lay a groundwork of trust, providing some assurance that we had no hidden agenda.

It was not long until a Chinese friend, another visiting professor at the University of Illinois, came to see us. The university had received our application and had contacted our friend in China, who had contacted the man now seated across from us. The university officials had one major concern: Did we understand that Peking University was not a religious institution and that we would not be free to use our classroom to promote our personal religious beliefs? Our applications' emphasis on the Christian aspect of our work was apparently quite clear to these officials!

Certainly, we responded, we understood that limitation, especially since in our own public schools, the same situation exists: Teachers cannot use their classrooms for religious indoctrination.

Okay, the visitor said, that was all he needed to know. The university definitely wanted us to come. It seemed that the credibility of our work with people in need outweighed any perceived disadvantage of our religious commitment.

In any case, in less than two years, the Yoking Map was no longer an abstract exercise and would soon be leading us halfway around the world!

4

China, *Hello!*

Experiencing the Yoking Map

There was a group of perhaps twenty men blocking the sidewalk. A few were kneeling down in a circle, absorbed in some game that involved playing pieces, while others stood over them or lounged against the wall. Although the sidewalk was broad, we would still have to walk right through them to reach our destination. We were in a part of Beijing that was unfamiliar to us. The city, being the national capital, was not unaccustomed to foreigners. However, we were going to visit a friend in her apartment and there were few *waiguoren* (literally, "outside-country-people," used to refer to foreigners) in this part of the city of nine million residents.

Without speaking to each other, we looked across the street. We could cross over and, once beyond the group blocking our current path, cross back to this side of the street. Later, in talking about this incident, we agreed that our low-level feeling of insecurity was not very realistic. We had been in the People's Republic of China for some months. We knew that there were strict gun laws and that this communist state did not flinch at enforcing its laws. We also knew that there were strong taboos about hassling foreigners, partly because of the practical consequence it would have of discouraging tourism. Actually, we always felt much safer walking around Chinese neighborhoods at night than we had felt back home.

Maybe it is always true in another country that one just doesn't know enough to be worried, but the public presence of uniformed army personnel in China gave us a sense of ever-present authority uncommon in the United States. So we generally felt unconcerned about our personal safety.

Still, China was changing so fast. Our tales of the China of 1986 were unrecognizable to an acquaintance who had left China in 1985. There was increasing freedom to speak out, and energy to begin new projects. We came to the conclusion that China in 1986 must be somewhat like our own country at the turn of the century: experiencing a great sense of progress and energetic activity.

This change did not seem entirely orderly. We would occasionally read of street vendors beating up government inspectors and soda-pop salesmen intimidating customers into paying inflated prices. These were always Chinese-to-Chinese encounters, however. The reports were generally in the form of news broadcasts or articles that would contain a moral lesson about how wrong such activities were and would emphasize the punishment being inflicted on the offenders. Even so, such incidents continued to happen.

There is something vaguely threatening about any group of men idly hanging around on a sidewalk. Therefore, we thought about crossing the street to avoid going through this group. The road was eight lanes wide. Traffic was sparse on this Sunday afternoon, but it was cold and we would be adding quite a distance to our walk. Again, without speaking and with a shrug of the shoulders, we agreed to forge ahead on this side of the street.

No one moved very much out of our way, so we tried to thread carefully among the bodies. Halfway through, we were directly crossing the line of vision of the tallest member of those assembled. He was leaning against the building, had longish hair and a leather jacket, indicating that he was likely an independent entrepreneur. There were rumors that some of these enterprising people worked just barely within the legal limits governing such activity, and some even dabbled in the black market we had heard about but never sought out. He didn't seem to pay attention to us, but suddenly we heard him say brightly in English, "Hello! How are you?"

We both stopped in our tracks and looked up at him, entirely astonished. He repeated the words, "Hello! How are you?" This time, we responded, "Hello! Fine, thank you, and you?" The man was smiling but seemed confused by our response. When he repeated his initial sentences, we quickly realized that they were the only English phrases he had picked up, probably from the radio. So we responded, "Hello!" and he smiled as broadly as we did. There was general happy approval murmured among the others who were now watching us. As we continued on, unable to resist turning back to look at the group a final time, several of them waved.

That interaction summarizes one aspect of our encounter with China. One authority has suggested that the United States-China relationship has been a series of ups and downs. Over the centuries, Americans have viewed China with emotions ranging from "admiration" to "contempt," from "compassion" to "fear," "disenchantment," and "hostility" toward "the yellow peril," until our current attitude seems to be stretched between "euphoria" and "skepticism."[1] In looking back, when we were in China during 1986, we were there at the height of euphoria on both sides. During that year, restrictions seemed the least oppressive, openness was becoming more possible, and rules that limited contact with foreigners were regularly being cancelled. The warm response we received from the leather-jacketed sidewalk lounger was typical of our experiences—reflecting the approach-avoidance scenario that has characterized Chinese-American relations.

A Land of Contrasts

There is a certain historical affinity between Americans and the Chinese that is difficult to explain, but we were in China long enough to appreciate one expert's warning about this apparent sense of commonality. In the aftermath of the Tiananmen Square incidents in June 1989, he wrote that we would do well to remember that the People's Republic is not America. That is, even such phrases as "democracy" and "freedom," which are held in esteem by members of both societies, can mean very different things in each culture.[2] We must not be misled into thinking that whatever differences there are between the two cultures are minor.

Therefore, having lived there only one year, we cannot presume to explain Chinese culture to you. Instead, we can share with you a few of our experiences that may give you limited insight into some aspects of the world's most populous nation.

China has always had a very mysterious aspect to it. Many people also automatically think of it as a beautiful land of contrasts. Both stereotypes are true. We saw many remarkable pagodas and ponds of lotuses, and we would walk through the Summer Palace and be astounded at the decadent luxury in evidence. The "long porch," a covered walkway, has, between each two supporting poles, a hand-painted scene from one of China's major novels. We looked in wonder at the boat of marble built by the Empress Dowager Ci Xi, who had used funds designated for the Chinese navy to provide herself with this elaborate retreat seven miles from the Forbidden City, city of the emperors.

Some of the twelve-foot statues guarding the entrances to Buddhist temples depicted angry and scowling spirits with bulging muscles and bared teeth. Carved gargoyles on granite balconies overlooked pink, red, and white blossoms on the carefully tended groves of trees lining the walk.

The cultural arts have always been important in China. We enjoyed the Beijing Opera, with its fanciful, bright-colored costumes and painted actors' faces, each "mask" having a traditional meaning. The singing we heard on the radio had that unique atonal quality that seems so exotic to the foreign ear. And the traditional acrobatic acts were amazing, stunning, and any other adjective P. T. Barnum might have been able to apply. Imagine watching a group of fifteen young women dressed in sparkling white outfits and bearing peacock feather fans, jumping on a single bicycle, one after the other, until all fifteen were balanced with their fans extended—producing a giant human peacock traveling the stage in circles! The *wushu* (kung fu) demonstrations were just as spellbinding.

Visitors also have a choice of gardens that belonged to the emperors. One, for example, allowed you to walk for a mile in an enclosed setting. (The emperor visited this garden only one day a year, on the winter solstice, to pray for good harvest. Another was reserved for planting prayers.) Or one might gaze with awe at the Buddha carved out of a mountain; four men can comfortably sit on the figure's toenail.

The river people, traveling in their junks, and plying their ancient trades, have changed their daily habits very little, regardless of the tumultuous decades of history that have swept over them this century.

The traveler to China is not disappointed, because all these exotic scenes are everywhere, not manufactured to attract tourism currency. Because they are a natural part of the fabric of this huge nation, the China of the mysterious Orient is still plainly evident.

But we found more modern aspects of China, too. There are the computer labs, where university students are working on advanced problems. In the cities, high-rise apartments, with laundry hanging on the balconies, are everywhere. Tall stone buildings, put up hurriedly in the last few years, came to seem much more typical of Chinese architecture than the pagodas we admired through filtered sunlight.

Stalls crowd the streets. In one city, one creative salesman sold pop and candy and had three phones for rent by the minute, since private telephones are a major luxury and no public telephone system exists.

We were amazed to find out that Chinese people are crazy about ice cream, even in winter! At a fair we visited, we obligingly downed the proffered ice cream bar, which we found awkward to eat with our gloves on. In the northeast, at the annual ice festival, we took a photo of a woman who was selling ice cream as she stood in padded, knee-high boots that must have been two inches thick all around!

It was very evident that China has limited resources to meet all the needs of its more than one billion people. Consider transportation. Bicycles travel the streets in crowds of hundreds, dodging traffic and bus drivers that might (or might not) be looking out for them. And the buses! It was not unusual for us to decide to wait for another bus, rather than try to cram onto one that already had people's arms sticking out the windows. But, as we would back away, several people behind us might well press on! Once or twice we even witnessed a strange ritual we had heard about. The bus would wait patiently, like a cow being milked, while kindhearted pedestrians would push on the backs of two or three people trying to squeeze on the bus. *Yi! Er! San!* they would yell. One! Two! Three!—and then they would push with all their might. After two or three such efforts, the last of the bodies would mash into those already on board and the doors would pop closed. The helpful assistants would walk away, laughing, and returning the friendly waves of those arms hanging out the windows.

Another source of culture shock to Americans, and other Westerners used to orderly queues, was the general absence of this polite custom in China. This was a reality that neither of us ever really adapted to, and we wondered why it had occurred. Some say that courtesy and etiquette were viewed with suspicion during the Cultural Revolution. Even anyone using "please" and "thank you" was reportedly considered too heavily influenced by the West, a punishable offense. Such niceties as lines disappeared as the tangled ethics of that chaotic time changed many aspects of Chinese life.

It may also be, at least in part, that the limited resources must be spread so sparingly among the vast populace that there is created a fierce determination to obtain what one needs. When relatively few buses compared to the large population are available, and long distances must be covered, potential passengers become desperate. Official policies indirectly fostered consumer assertiveness. We came to view lack of service as typical in the government shops and agencies, which meant that one had to be insistent to be waited on by the clerk, who might be chatting with friends, confident she would be paid, whether or not she sold anything that day.

Ignorance Abroad

Our lack of coping ability in China sometimes proved comical. For example, it became usual for the clerks at the campus post office to call us forward when we needed to buy stamps. They would talk a little English and we would talk a little Chinese, but they would wait on us promptly, even while we could hear comments about *waiguoren* being murmured by other customers. Those complainers were probably grumbling about the seemingly special treatment we foreigners were receiving. The postal clerks had begun this practice after one of us had stood for twenty minutes in a chaotic "line" to buy stamps. The mass of people in front never decreased, because new people would always crush in front of anyone patiently waiting. It was obviously out of pure pity that the clerks waited on us quickly!

There was also the time in the train dining car. Usually we traveled first class ("soft sleeper"), using the money from our teaching salaries. After nearly being mauled as we tried to exit one "hard-seat" train car—those coming on refused to wait for those disembarking—a sense of panic set in, and we decided first class was not a luxury but a necessity, since we had not yet adapted to this crushing cultural aspect of China. However, on this one trip, there were no soft-sleeper seats to be had. (The Chinese could buy these coveted tickets through their workplaces. Some enterprising people now earned enough to afford them and had the connections to get them.) We did not really mind traveling "hard sleeper," since we still had a berth to lie down on. It also let us visit with interesting people, which this time included two workers in a joint-venture Jeep factory.

This class of travel meant that no train personnel came to ask us what we would like to eat and then escort us to the dining car before it was opened to the general public. The loudspeaker, standard equipment in each train compartment, had been blaring a variety of music, some of which we recognized from their styles as patriotic songs or Hong Kong pop. Suddenly there came a garbled announcement. Our traveling companions led us to understand that the dining car was open. We wandered back and waited at the door for a seat. People pushed past us, even though the car was full. Then they would stand intimidatingly over a diner, who would hurry and clear out of the seat. We became indignant after the third, fourth, and fifth person pushed past us to grab the available spots while we stood there hungry. Finally, we began to block the doorway to prevent anyone else passing (even a father trying to join his ten-year-old daughter, who was saving him a seat. Of course, we did not understand this at the time, and apologized as best we could later). As people would try to get around us, the two of us formed a human blockade and were quite pleased with our success, in spite of the growing rumblings of complaint behind us.

Soon a burly soldier stood up from his seat and came over to us. He talked very fast in Chinese, so we put on our usual smiles and used the all-important *Ting bu dong* ("Hear but not understand"). As he talked a little more intensely and louder, we kept pleasantly responding *Ting bu dong*. To his credit, he laughed. Then, gently taking our arms, he encouraged us to step forward. Meanwhile, one of the kitchen workers was frantically ousting two diners, and the soldier seemed relieved when the woman came over to guide us to those seats. She indicated that she wanted us to order, but we shrugged our shoulders. In exasperation, she waved her hands all over the car, thus suggesting we should point out what we wanted. We happily pointed to several diners' plates.

From our new perspective, it suddenly struck us that we had caused a near riot by not understanding the standard procedures. Now we watched patrons enter the dining car and go to the back near the kitchen to order their food. Having ordered, they would then stand by the table of the person who seemed most likely to be done first. By the time the newcomers could sit down, their food would be brought to them. We had seen these people standing over diners, but had not understood that this was the accepted routine.

We were feeling rather silly by this time. If we had known enough Chinese, we would have stood up and apologized to everyone in general. However, they all seemed to think it was quite comical, and probably only one or two had taken real offense. When the worker brought our meal, she also brought one very tarnished and smudgy fork and a spoon in the same condition, both probably dug out of some forgotten shelf. She must have assumed we were so very "foreign" that we would be totally unable to use chopsticks! Trying to salvage a little bit of dignity, one of us used our best Chinese to say, "We don't know how to speak Chinese, but we can eat Chinese." As we proudly demonstrated our skill to her, her smile indicated that we had been forgiven.

We were always grateful for the good humor with which our friends and students, and the strangers we no doubt offended, tolerated our blundering. Certainly, there was the occasional person who seemed to hate foreigners on sight, like the elderly woman who walked by mumbling in such an angry fashion that our ears would probably have been scorched if we knew that vocabulary. Another older woman sitting on her camp stool on the sidewalk, whom we approached for directions, stared steadily in front of her, not acknowledging our existence. We had asked her for directions several times in our poor Chinese, trying to get her attention, when it finally occurred to us that she might really want us just to leave her alone. Who knows what pain these aged beings have experienced in China's sometimes violent past?

Merging the Old and the New

Most of the time, we were delighted to discover that Americans and Chinese have a similar sense of humor. Perhaps this is one reason for our affinity. We learned that TVs had become generally available around 1984, and now it seemed that many people in the cities owned one. The programming had produced new crazes, like "cross-talk" teams. Although we watched the countless Bud Abbott/Lou Costello-type teams that appeared on television with a total lack of comprehension, we were confident that these routines varied little from those that had entertained us at home.

Another remarkable aspect of Chinese TV was the popularity of soap operas, considering that the Cultural Revolution had ended merely a decade before and that Western visitors were still not very common. Although many cities in China are still off-limits to foreigners, Japanese and Mexican soap operas that dealt with betrayal and murder were in vogue. Many young women had their hair styled like one of the characters.

One comment about TVs: While it seemed that many people in the cities had them—we walked down one alley of one-room row houses and found a family with the TV perched on a camp stool as they sat on the bricks in the road—we assumed correctly that such conveniences were not as common in the rural areas. As of the end of 1984, 68 percent of China's population still lived in rural areas[3] or "the countryside." Of those people, close to 45 percent had no access to electricity as of 1986.[4] China is working hard to establish some basic living standards in terms of electricity and full-scale public-schooling for whole sections of its population.

It was refreshing that adultery was not included in the list of sins on the TV shows. This fact was consistent with the Victorian morals that seemed to permeate the society. Because it was our first experience in such an innocent culture, we found ourselves a little shocked to see two grown men, or two teenage boys, walking unconcernedly hand-in-hand down the street. But, because sex was such a strong taboo, there was not the slightest hint of impropriety—or political statement—about such actions. Ironically, a certain freedom accompanies these social prohibitions.

Some Chinese youth may be too anxious to change these "old ways." Yes, some students told us, they hope to be as free as Americans someday. They went on to provide an example of what they saw as American freedom: one day they will be able to live together before marriage and no one can "give them problems." Oh! we found ourselves replying, if only you knew the grief that so many have experienced through such license, you might be less quick to abandon what you have.

We found many such conflicts between traditional values and encroaching progress. Ancient temples continued their vigils under skies increasingly polluted by industrial growth. Because there was a greater demand for the electricity than current systems could support, there were brown-outs and even no-electricity days. Small traditional row houses not only provided living space, but preserved a sort of ecosystem supported by the limited water and the local public toilets and showers. In this type of environment, communities of neighbors had survived generations. But many of these small houses were now being razed so that tall apartment complexes could be built, which would stress the water supply, the toilets, the showers, and would eliminate neighborhoods that had existed since the time of the emperors. Groaning and stretching at the seams, the Chinese challenge continues to be how to keep the best of the old even while embracing the useful parts of what is new.

Lessons in Hospitality

We were often humbled by the kindness shown to us in China. With some shame, we began to comment to ourselves that we were learning more about hospitality in this communist country than from what we had experienced—and sometimes extended—back home.

A strange thing about Chinese culture is that the same lady who would jab your ribs to get on the bus first might also get off at your stop rather than hers and go blocks out of her way if you asked her for directions. Apparently, in Chinese culture, family and those with power over you matter a great deal, while strangers in general do not. However, when we came into a stranger's realm of responsibility—by asking for directions, for example—we found that person willing to be of as much help as possible.

Consider our travel experiences. Our friends in Beijing were a little worried about our plans to travel China on our own (with some justification, as a few of our adventures would indicate). And so, one or the other would suggest an acquaintance of theirs to contact in various cities. In one particular case, a Beijing friend contacted a college classmate then living in a city we were planning to visit. She apparently asked him to help us get situated in a hotel and also asked for his aid in getting coveted tickets for one of the boats that travel down the Yangtze River.

This man and his young daughter met us at the train and took us to a lovely hotel. He visited with us for a while and then took us down the street to eat at a shop it would have been difficult for us to find by ourselves. Finally, he apologized for having to leave us. It seemed that he was convening a national conference on acid rain, and scientists were arriving from all over China that day. He had taken two hours off from his duties to welcome us, but he really had to go. We were embarrassed at this level of kindness, but he assured us that he was happy to be of help. Then he told us he had arranged for a translator to spend the following day with us. That next evening, he arrived at our hotel with tickets for the boat. He had spent the whole day giving presentations at his conference and had not even taken the time to eat before he came over to launch us safely on our way. We were dumbfounded. "Why," we found ourselves asking, "would you go to all this trouble for strangers?" He looked at us blankly. The fact that his college friend had asked him seemed to be reason enough.

Another friend of ours appeared tired one day. We asked her why. She told us that two of her friends had arrived at her door around eight o'clock the night before and stayed until eleven. After she sat and visited with them, she still had to prepare for a full teaching schedule the next day. She never considered any option but to entertain her friends, who had ridden two hours by bike across the city on the chance she would be available for a visit. It did not occur to her to complain about the situation; in fact, she indicated how much she had enjoyed her friends' visit. This same friend had faithfully invited us to share every holiday and every Saturday night with her family, just because we were strangers in her land.

We began to wonder how much we have lost in our own society, where it is now advisable to phone first before visiting, in case your targeted hosts would rather see a particular TV show instead. Perhaps, as these "modern conveniences" become more common in China, the warm openness we experienced might disappear there as well. But, for now, we felt vaguely that we were being reminded of an important quality of life that we had misplaced in our own busy schedules.

The Winds of Change

Why should it have surprised us that people in China wanted basically the same things we do? Whenever they had the opportunity, people would eagerly purchase Japanese cameras and American jeans. Although these products were not generally available, they had great appeal, because decades of communist rule had not eliminated the appetite for imported goods and status symbols. Coming from one of the most materialistic societies on the planet, we cannot possibly stand in judgment of them. Still, we *were* surprised. Maybe, at some level, we had believed the propaganda of the "new man" of China. Perhaps we attributed noble forbearance to all the world's poor, as if they really did not mind doing without the luxuries we considered to be daily necessities. If it is true that these people would like lifestyles as comfortable as ours, there are some important implications for how we approach partnerships with people in other lands. We will have to be open-minded about the directions in which they want to go. Here, too, we must keep learning the deeper and deeper meanings of Jesus' instruction to "love your neighbor as yourself."

You may sense that we regret certain of the changes taking place in China. That, no doubt, comes from our own selfishness. But it is not our place to wish China would stay the same so that we can have a welcome refuge from the materialistic, oversexed culture that we inhabit, a culture we would not trade permanently, although we might like to retreat from it every once in a while. The fact that China is changing is a given, and one we can do nothing about but accept.

Certainly, all the changes are not bad, and many of them will come through the young, as is common in every society. One of the greatest delights of our time in China was our students. They were open and energetic. They were also funny; both they and we were relieved to find out we all liked to laugh. The students rarely wore traditional blue Mao jackets, although sometimes they did because these clothes were subsidized and therefore plentiful. More often, they wore jogging suits, with which the females would wear high heels. The women sometimes wore blouses and skirts, and we were amazed at the skill with which they managed bicycles while dressed this way. The males usually wore jeans, which were highly prized, or slacks and bright shirts. This was a change. Only a few years before, one student told us, the shirt factories had only been allowed to manufacture shirts in light blue and white.

At first we had to work to encourage class participation. We learned that a proverb taught early on was "The first bird out of the woods gets shot." These were the children raised during the Cultural Revolution, and they had probably seen this proverb proven true. Still, as trust among us grew, they participated more and more. In fact, we had to be careful. At one point, enthusiasm for a play script being developed almost produced a new teaching technique, English-by-chaos: all the students shout whatever they want as long as it is in English!

More often, they would participate in orderly discussions, and here we found some of our most surprising facts. In "Red China," most of the university males did not want to marry university women "because when you educate women, you create trouble." In one class, several girls renounced a desire for an elaborate wedding, which can cost a fortune. Such weddings are just coming back into vogue after being abolished with the founding of the People's Republic. The teacher's approving nods stopped in surprise as the women added that they would rather their future husbands spend the money on a long honeymoon journey!

The students were sometimes open in a shy way, innocently making disarming comments, like the student who raised his hand in class and said sincerely when called on, "You're doing a wonderful job." These young people were generally attuned to new ideas, and we saw some of the early sprouts of what would be termed "the democracy movement" three years later. In one class, a student would occasionally burst out with the English word "Democracy!" while thrusting his fist in the air. His fellow classmates would quickly shush him.

One English discussion in another class was especially touching. A different team of students proposed the topics for each session, and one issue to be examined was "What would you do if you were chairman of the department?" There was a hush over the room. Finally one student ventured to give an answer, but he was almost immediately cut off by an outburst from one of his angry peers. "What gives you the right to imagine what you would do as chairman?" he shouted, apparently threatened by this deviation from the traditional unquestioning acceptance of authority. The first student was flustered, and his mouth worked in silence for a moment. He seemed to be searching for the proper English words, and then he blurted out, "The Consti-, the Consti-," until he finally had the whole word in mind, "The Constitution!"

He was partly correct. The Constitution of 1982 does protect many rights by allowing practices previously forbidden. What this student did not reflect on, and what became clear in June 1989, is that Article 28 of that same document defines the role of the "state" to be one that "maintains public order and suppresses treasonable and other counter-revolutionary activities," without outlining who gets to decide just what "counter-revolutionary" means.[5] As we watch developments in this dynamic country and try to reach out in Jesus' name in a helpful fashion, we should remember the admonition that China is not America.

The Church in China

Into this millennia-old culture, with its dramatic history during this century, the Christian church has been introduced several times. Three times over the centuries, the church has planted seeds in China's culture, and twice its influence disappeared. In A.D. 635, the Nestorians came, but they vanished by the 900s. The Franciscans worked from 1294 to 1398, leaving no traces of common practice of the faith. The third phase began in 1601 with the arrival of the Jesuits, who began to be joined by Protestants in 1807.[6]

After 1949, restrictions on religion were common during the early years of the People's Republic, although some religious activity continued. Foreign missionaries had generally left or been forced out by 1951, and the Chinese set about producing an "authentically Chinese" Christian church. Before the revolution—or "liberation," as it is commonly referred to in China—most people practiced traditional folk religions, with Buddhists claiming the largest organized membership. After that time, the majority of the population was officially "nonreligious." All during this period, the Christian church attracted less than 1 percent of the population.[7]

Western observers had thought that even this tiny enclave had been wiped out during the years of the Cultural Revolution. As in the case of the Boxer Rebellion at the beginning of the twentieth century,[8] an anti-Western hysteria swept the country in 1966. Unlike the period of the Boxer Rebellion, the Red Guard who carried out this later campaign succeeded broadly and gained control of all the major institutions. Universities were closed, their professors terrorized or sent to the countryside for "reeducation." Schoolchildren went to classes mainly to criticize their teachers. As China withdrew from international contacts, church property was confiscated, books and other possessions were burned, and all religious meetings were prohibited.

During this time, with no accurate reports to guide them, some observers in the West concluded that China was merely going through a creative period of development.[9] Once the extent of the terror and confusion of those years began to leak out, outsiders looked on in horrified wonder. One source comments, "As late as the summer of 1979, a Protestant mission executive wrote that 'organized Christianity in the People's Republic of China, has, as far as we can see, disappeared.'"[10]

Then, in September 1979, the church felt the thawing of government policies that was becoming evident in other areas of society. The first official Christian services were allowed at the Mo En (formerly Moore Memorial) Church in Shanghai. That day, five-thousand worshipers crowded into two services.[11] As time went on, it became apparent that the church had not only survived, but had actually flourished in small-group settings throughout the country.

During our year in China, we attended a small Protestant church in the neighborhood of Peking University that had opened only six months before we arrived. Warmly welcomed, we faithfully went to services, even though we could not understand the hour-long sermons until we arranged for an interpreter during the second term. We were immediately enfolded in Christian warmth. We saw many older people there, and not a few younger people, too. Even though we would be told, "Young people do not attend church," we could look around and see that they did. In time, we came to recognize this apparent contradiction as very Chinese. As far as we could gather, if young people attended church, it was all right, as long as no one made a big deal out of it. Perhaps if the church were to force the government to take notice by bragging about how many young people came, the government would "lose face," with negative consequences to follow. In any case, despite the official statement that young people did not attend, the church welcomed anyone who wanted to come.

We gained another insight into the church in China over the issue of baptism. At Easter, several adults were sprinkled as they joined the official communion of the church. "Ah," we concluded, "the church in China has come down on the side of sprinkling." But in June, the front floor tiles of the church were removed, revealing a tub. This baptistry was filled with bucket after bucket of water, hand-carried during the two-hour service. Then over twenty people were immersed. We quickly grabbed an English-speaking Chinese acquaintance and hurried toward the pastor after service to find out how they could sprinkle at Easter and immerse in June. "Where does the church in China stand on baptism?" we asked.

The pastor smiled kindly as he explained that the church is not heated except by coal stoves; so they sprinkled at Easter when it was so cold, but immersion was available in the summer! He went on to say that because the Protestant church in China now combines people from many traditions, a choice of baptismal methods is offered whenever possible.

At a Catholic service we attended while in China, we were surprised to hear the service conducted in Latin! It seems that the Chinese Catholic Patriotic Association had split with the Vatican before the Vatican II Council. The issues included the Vatican's recognition of Taiwan and the ordination of bishops.[12]

A Spiritual Journey

During the last six weeks we were in China, in early 1987, we traveled over ten thousand miles around the country. This was just after the New Year's demonstrations that led to Hu Yaobang's ultimate dismissal, which eventually served as the setting event of the democracy movement two years later. It appears providential that we were able to journey at that time. An uprising in Tibet closed that area to visitors sporadically after we were there. Furthermore, the entire tenor of society changed during the "anti-bourgeoise liberalization" campaign that followed the initial student demonstrations in the winter of 1986–1987.

Our goal was to see as many areas of China as possible. In addition, we had a list of most of the Protestant seminaries then open and wanted to visit them. We also visited Catholic churches when we were able.

In Nanjing, we had the opportunity to visit with Han Wenzao, general secretary of the Amity Foundation and also of the China Christian Council. The Nanjing Union Theological Seminary which had been shut down during the Cultural Revolution, reopened in 1981. The seminary complex houses both the theological school and offices of the Amity Foundation.

Han Wenzao was most gracious during our visit. When we asked about the priorities of the church in China, he said that a major challenge is to maintain the church's unique Chinese character so that Christianity would never again appear to be a "foreign religion." Because so many Christians suffered along with other people during the persecutions of the Cultural Revolution, those terrible years are now seen as a refining fire for the church. Even non-Christians now perceived the church in China as an institution that had come through the same difficulty as they did and therefore belonged to their culture. Han Wenzao was very concerned that this painfully won credibility not be tarnished by carelessly allowing domination by Christians in the West. Yet, he assured us, there was no desire to deny the international nature of Christianity. The challenge was to integrate the two branches of the church.

We found ourselves asking about church goals at each of the eight seminaries we visited. At one school, the pastor could quickly list his hopes for the church:

1. Training more pastors, to make up for the "lost generation" who could not be trained during the Cultural Revolution (Almost all of the trained pastors active in 1986 were in their sixties, seventies, and even eighties.)
2. Printing more Christian literature
3. Undertaking social projects that would aid in the development of China, thus enhancing the church's identity as a valuable institution
4. Increasing contact with the Western church

At another seminary, we found a delightful young couple who were especially concerned about training a sufficient number of teachers and pastoral leaders. They had been in the first graduating class after Nanjing Union Theological Seminary reopened and had married right after graduation, leaving immediately to become founding faculty at the seminary where they now taught.

Another pastor who shared the same concern voiced his fear that the church in the countryside would begin to combine Christian doctrine with folk religions and lose touch with historical Christian theology if religious leaders could not be trained fast enough.

At a fourth seminary, an elderly woman quickly responded to our question in excellent English. "Unity" was her hope for the church in China. "Pray for us," she asked. And then she commented, "But I think you struggle with the question of unity in America, too, don't you?" We assured her that we did.

After another seminary professor reflected on our question, she expressed the hope that China would soon be able to contribute to world theology out of its experience. We encouraged her enthusiastically, having already concluded that we had a great deal to learn from these Christian brothers and sisters who had survived so much and had gained new strength as a result of their trials.

We cannot shed much light on the role that unregistered house churches play in China, mainly because our time in China had been arranged at the initiative of individual Chinese people. Since all our actions would be seen as reflecting on them, we felt obligated to conduct ourselves in such a way that our behavior in our role as guests was above reproach. Thus, while we asked people we met about the house churches and their relationship to the registered church in China, we did not seek out any worship services.

There is some discussion in the United States about whether the officially recognized church works comfortably with the house churches. We wondered if some of the house churches exist in opposition to the registered church because they believe the government interferes too much. Several people we talked to agreed that there are still incidents of religious persecution. This fact has to do, at least in part, with the way the People's Republic is organized. The provincial, regional, and local government may or may not adhere to all the official policies, although in theory each level carries out national decrees. Even though the stated position in Beijing may be to tolerate the free practice of religion, a local administrator may ignore this policy and cause great grief to local Christians, whether in the house churches or in the registered church. However, this sort of inconsistent treatment is not limited only to the church; reports of intellectuals being harassed also surface occasionally.

Of course, our own history of enforcing the civil rights of African-Americans—with some states and local communities actively resisting national policy—should contribute to our understanding of how such unjust conditions can exist. Even so, various people in the West have been advised by sources they trust that there are serious problems in regard to the free practice of the house churches and the credibility of the registered church. Although we cannot provide new insights for you, we can say that we observed sincere Christians every week for the year we attended a registered church in China. We talked openly with church leaders we met, and they seemed forthright with us.

It was sobering for us to talk with these people at seminary after seminary and hear of their struggles during the Cultural Revolution. We learned about the patience it took to work through elaborate and sometimes resistant channels to regain confiscated buildings—in one case, room by room—from the factories or schools that had taken possession of the buildings during those troubled times. The young seminary students we talked to in one city faced years of rigorous schooling, the prospect of low salaries, and a long period of service before they could be ordained. Some of them had left good jobs, and at least one talked of the discrimination he experienced because of his choice.

But there was never a complaining spirit among these Christian brothers and sisters. They were sharing their experiences as a natural part of their Christian discipleship, and all seemed to have the peace that comes from trusting God. When we speculated about a Chinese contribution to world theology, we guessed that the rich heritage of those years of suffering would have a lot to teach us. Although confused by where the house churches fit in, and not denying the fact that Christianity could be facing very difficult situations in China, we still found ourselves having a deep and warm response to the Christians we met. It is one more part of China that seemed too unfamiliar for us to fully comprehend.

Perhaps the only additional comment we can offer is to repeat what one young seminary teacher said. We have continued to correspond with her and were even able to entertain her in our home several years after our visit with her in China. At that time, since we thought we would surely never see her again, we figured that it was a valuable opportunity to obtain a response to an important question. Therefore, we boldly asked her if she was aware that some people in the United States would think she could not really be a Christian because she was associated with the registered church.

She sighed and nodded. Yes, she had heard that, she said, but she really didn't understand it. From her point of view, she went on, the church in China has neither power nor influence nor money. "If people come to church in China, it is because they want God. He is the only thing we have to offer them."

A Retrospective

You will recall that the idea of area-to-area matching led Christians in Champaign-Urbana to establish an ongoing relationship with a church agency in Northeast Brazil that we personalized by visiting the region. Taking that strategy one step farther, we created a Yoking Map, which matched Christians in every county of the United States with a particular area of the world. That map sparked our special interest in China, because so many states were matched with it, including Illinois. Then we ended up living for a year in China.

What have we learned from these adventures?

One thing we conclude is that we can generalize certain aspects of our experiences. The need to be servants not bosses, partners not providers—which we learned in our visit to Brazil—was a critical lesson as we made contact with the church in China. We learned firsthand that poverty in some countries is widespread and devastating, and we came to care about people facing desperate conditions. This personal empathy constantly renews our energy to keep trying to make a difference.

We also saw that the national church leaders we met were very competent people whom we could and *should* trust to develop strategies for the churches in their own countries. Because these leaders understood the history, culture, and needs of their people far better than we ever could, we realized we could learn a great deal from them.

We also learned that it would be hard for one person to be a specialist in both Brazil and China. Since the problems these countries face are very different, the strategies for the church and church agencies must be unique to each situation. Trying to apply to Brazil a strategy found effective in post-revolutionary China would be ridiculous. Both the Brazilian and Chinese cultures are far more complex than we could grasp in a two-week or even one-year visit. In both cases, our learning adventure has only just begun and will require some specialization.

As we reflect on our travels, we conclude that there is great practical wisdom in the area-to-area idea. Our year in China allowed us to develop a deep respect for the country, for its history and culture, and for the Christians there. But we were in China long enough to discover some things, like the crowds on the buses that could drive one crazy—and some aspects of their world view that would take years for us to begin to understand.

Our short visit to Brazil was enough to convince us of the value of personal encounters. The trip instilled in us a joy in knowing the agency personnel and a respect for their bravery in facing sometimes overwhelming odds while they try to change the conditions of the people they serve. The Brazilian people we met in the villages were warm and made us feel like family. The ongoing correspondence with our agency partners continues to give us new insights. A second delegation went to Brazil from the churches in Champaign-Urbana in 1989, and they returned with the same enthusiasm we felt after our own trip.

Our experience with church people, through working in-depth in Champaign-Urbana for twenty years and interacting with congregation members in other cities, makes us confident that Christians throughout the United States want to make a real difference in the world as faithful disciples of Christ. Yet, we must realize that we cannot reach all humanity directly. But how exciting it is to be part of the larger body! Think of what could happen if each part did its share. The power of people getting to know people has not been sufficiently tapped among Christians here at home. We have not yet seen what we can really do if we decided to live up to our potential as faithful followers of Jesus Christ.

5
Crosstown Bridges

Addressing Local Needs

$\mathcal{T}$here's something about visiting foreign countries that is really so exciting. Even the food differences are adventuresome, though you don't always want to know what you're eating. The postage stamps are often remarkable little glimpses into an unfamiliar and exotic way of life. The music is attractive just because it's not like anything we normally listen to at home.

Why is it that this same positive fascination doesn't extend across town? Too often, it would seem, the differences of these neighbors seem threatening and not at all intriguing. We are not as concerned about meeting these people and learning the reasons for their cultural practices as we are about making sure those practices don't bother us.

Maybe the last point is part of the answer. Our crosstown neighbors are close enough to have an impact on our daily lives. If we decide we don't like their food, their mannerisms, their music, we can't escape them by returning home, the way we can when we're overseas. We already *are* home, part of the same community.

We have a shared history with the people around us, not all of it good. There's been a lot of pain in that history, and communication has never been effectively developed between certain groups. For example, we may be involved directly in power struggles with our local neighbors over who controls the school board and what is the best use of public resources. It may be easier to get to know and appreciate people ten thousand miles away than those who live ten blocks away. Sometimes it seems that the distance between the suburbs and the inner city must be greater than the "great chasm" that separated Abraham and the beggar Lazarus from the rich man described in Luke 16:19–31.

As we consider how to be faithful followers of Jesus Christ in terms of how we spend our resources, we cannot ignore that there are needs in our own communities in addition to those around the world. Although the desperate conditions of our international neighbors demand our active response, that response should not be at the expense of the concern we show for those across town.

The Problem of Poverty

There have been many traditional outreaches to the poor, both church-sponsored and secular. Missions were providing hot meals and beds decades before the current increased concern for the homeless developed. Government agencies are providing aid to families with dependent children, as well as to the disabled. If this support is not enough, and it rarely is, a whole system of voluntary private agencies provides second-string support.

Still, poverty continues to exist. And changing circumstances in society may have the greatest impact on those who are most vulnerable. Policies for housing development and the treatment of those with mental problems have been revised over the years, and the consequences are evident in the worsening condition of the homeless. Welfare reform tries to meet immediate needs, and yet people argue over whether the financial assistance actually helps the recipients or encourages dependency. Drugs enslave whole neighborhoods and spread throughout the broader community, threatening the fabric of the entire society.

Jesus said, "The poor you will always have with you" (Matt. 26:11). His statement of fact might be most accurately understood in the context of Deuteronomy 15, from which he was quoting. There, Moses announces the canceling of all debts every seven years (v. 1). But he also indicates that there would be no poor among the people of God if they obeyed God's commandments (vv. 4–5). Just a few verses later, however, Moses declares that, in fact, the poor will always be in the land, and so people are commanded "to be openhanded toward your brothers and toward the poor and needy in your land" (v. 11). Although there would be no poor if the Israelites were careful to follow God's commands, it was only realistic to have announced a back-up policy if they chose not to follow though.

When Jesus says there will always be poor among us, he is probably acknowledging the human factor in an imperfect world. There will always be people who are weaker and are at the margins of society, people who just can't make it on their own, whether through problems of addiction or dependency or because of physical or mental limitations. He is no doubt also recognizing the fact that injustice will continue until the end of time, that even his most faithful servants will live in societies with limited fairness, that certain groups of people will always have problems. If so, he would not be misleading us.

Even in the first years of the life of the church we are part of today, there was dissension about the equitable distribution of food to the Greek- and Hebrew-speaking widows (Acts 6:1).

Whether it is because there will always be weaker people, or because injustice is too deeply ingrained in the social environments we create and maintain, it seems evident that the poor will always be with us. To date, society has tried a variety of strategies, but conditions seem to worsen. Maybe it's time to explore a more effective approach.

Personalized Outreach

When, in previous chapters, we outlined our ideas for meeting the needs of our international neighbors, we stressed the importance of establishing ongoing relationships that would make our outreach more meaningful and the distribution of our available resources more effective. The Yoking Map was suggested as a strategy to encourage area-to-area global understanding—a way to translate the noble but abstract idea of "Christian charity" into practical specifics.

Because this regional approach will make an area's needs more understandable, it can increase a congregation's motivation to participate in benevolent efforts overseas. For example, we might want to challenge Jane Doe to limit her luxury spending (which in her case goes toward buying a new outfit every month) on behalf of others. One way would be to appeal to her compassionate instincts by telling her that she could "help people" in, say Bangladesh, by redirecting a portion of her inflated clothing budget to address their *general* needs. But, unless Jane has some emotional ties with these people and understands *how* her money might help, she is quite likely to feel that making her own fashion statement is more important than addressing the desperate condition of faceless residents in a distant land. On the other hand, if Jane is told about the work of a church agency in Bangladesh and knew that her funds would buy chickens to help single mothers start a cottage industry, she may willingly limit her clothing expenditure—especially if a member of her congregation has just returned from visiting the fledgling poultry farms and explained exactly how important this project really is. Our challenge to this sister in Christ then has some depth to it.

The question before us, as we consider a domestic strategy, is whether a similar matching that establishes personal relationships might be a helpful approach between Christians who possess "extra" resources and people in need in their local communities.

As we noted earlier, it may actually be more difficult to build a bridge of understanding between some sections of a local community than between one town or area of the United States and another country. As one young woman we know observed about the challenge of addressing local poverty, "It all seems pretty unreal to those of us out here in the suburbs." However, if we would be faithful disciples, we cannot ignore our local communities. We need to bring the same creativity, determination, and hope to the challenge to be servants at home that we bring to our international partnerships.

Precisely because the needs in your local community might be more threatening to your own sense of well-being, the idea of relationships could be all the more important. It is too easy to ignore "the poor" if those two words seem to lump a whole lot of individuals into a faceless blob. Categorizing groups of people robs them of their individual traits and gifts. If we are put off by the idea of making overtures to a large group of needy people in our local communities, maybe we would find just one person approachable.

We found this idea helpful in our works through *empty tomb*. One example stands out in our minds. A certain congregation shared the distrust of "the poor" and "those on welfare" that is common among those removed from the situation. The church's leaders did not particularly promote this attitude, but it was an inherited perception that came as naturally to the parishioners as being a fan of the hometown team does to residents of any given city.

After some urging, this church got involved with our food-delivery program. We do not see *empty tomb* as a social agency that "takes care of the poor" on behalf of the larger society. Rather, we define our organization as "serving the whole church as it serves others." We see ourselves as building bridges between individuals in need and those people in churches who want to help. Therefore, our food work is organized in such a way that other organizations call our office with the names of people who have requested help with food. We then call a congregational representative, who will arrange for someone from his or her church to deliver food to a specific family or individual.

The people referred to us may have run short at the end of the month, or may have had a family emergency (as major as a funeral, with droves of visiting relatives to feed, or as "minor"—but still important—as having to use the last of the month's food stamps to buy the ingredients for a cake to send to the school bake sale so a son does not feel left out). Or a family may have fallen through the cracks of the social welfare system—they qualify for food stamps or other assistance, but the father lost his job this week and it takes some time to process the necessary paperwork. We accept these calls because Jesus has commanded us to care about everyone, with no distinction made as to whether they are the "deserving poor" or not (Luke 6:32–36).

We referred a number of different families to this initially skeptical church. Soon we were hearing comments like: "Well, I don't know about *all* the poor, but I've met one mother who is working as many hours as she can get as a hotel maid. When there are no football weekends, she gets less work but not more food stamps for her family. She's really trying, and I'm glad we could help."

"I don't know about all the poor . . ." Another beam has been laid in the foundation of that bridge of understanding.

Longer-Term Solutions

While food deliveries are effective, as are clothing and furniture distribution, home repair, and many of the other works that *empty tomb* and similar groups provide in direct service to poor people, these responses deal with immediate needs. It is appropriate to help those in need make it through today or give them shelter for tonight. But how are we to cooperate in their efforts to set and achieve goals that will change their situations enough so that they can provide their own housing or food, a week or a year or five years from now?

The answer to that question is as varied as the individuals involved. Some need only a boost to get back on their feet. More than once we have received donations of food from a person or family "paying us back" for the help we gave them in a specific crisis. "You helped me, and I wish you would pass this on to someone who needs it now," they will say.

Others, with a little encouragement and effort, can gain the skills they lack if they have access to schooling, tutoring, or job training. Connections are an important resource. For example, you probably know many people who find summer jobs for their kids, but that is difficult if there is no parent who can arrange such opportunities. When we approached one businessman about providing summer employment for a young fellow who really wanted to work, the man said he reserved his summer jobs for students on athletic scholarships from the university. Although this man is to be commended because he was already helping lower-income kids through these jobs, the student athletes had that job connection because of their ability in sports. The young man we were trying to help had neither a father who could find him a job nor the skill to put points on a scoreboard. A bridge of Christian partnership would have been able to help him acquire the connections and introductions his natural circumstances did not provide. To his credit, this young man did not give up, but pursued one lead after another until he was working his way up to a management position in a pizza chain. Others in similar circumstances get discouraged and give up trying to insert themselves into what seems like a society labeled "for members only."

Other people who are presently in need have been affected so negatively by long-term poverty that it will take concentrated effort for them to change their established patterns. We have lived in a publicly subsidized, low-income housing project for the past decade. During that time we have seen many children grow up and start their own families, as is typical of most neighborhoods. When we see one generation after another settling into a pattern of receiving public assistance, it occurs to us that these kids are not really aware that there is an alternative to this sort of lifestyle for them.

Consider one friend we have helped over the years. One time she came to us promising that if we could help her out with some money for meat "just this last time," she would be all right, since next week she expected to get her food stamps. She told us that her oldest son had quit school and was living by his wits on the streets. Since he was not in school, he had been cut out of her public-aid grant and food-stamp allotment, decreasing the total amount the mother received. When this youth got especially hungry, he would break into the family apartment and eat as much as he wanted, literally taking the food out of his younger siblings' mouths. Because of our long relationship with this woman and a low level of mutual accountability that had developed during that time, it did not seem inappropriate for us to ask how getting stamps the following week would help, since it was likely her son would again break into her apartment and start the cycle all over again.

Our friend was amazed at the question, and her answer spoke volumes about her attitude toward life. She actually sounded a little condescending as she replied, "Why, it's always better when you get your stamps!" Her cycle of poverty did not even seem like a cycle to her. She had learned not to think beyond the day her food stamps arrived. If her son broke into her apartment next month, she would deal with that problem next month. In her mind, her only task was to survive until "next week."

People like this lady, whose lives consist of one survival challenge after another, will not be able to respond to a program that requires practiced, basic skills of long-term planning and goal setting. This woman and others like her will have to learn to look at the world in a whole new way. Someone from the outside needs to enter her experience and build up enough trust to introduce some very "foreign" ideas that deal with planning a better future. Someone will need to stand with her until survival does not seem like an elusive reality. In our culture of instant gratification, there may be fewer and fewer people who can actually guide this woman out of the patterns that bind her in continuing poverty, but if such people exist, they may well be in the church.

This sense of helplessness has tragic dimensions, as we learned from another woman we knew over a period of years. We had few experiences in common, but we would talk about those that are typical in any human existence: the weather, schools, parenting. Or we would just listen as she talked about her life and tried to sort some of it out.

This lady educated us as to how otherwise manageable circumstances can seem overwhelming as one is worn down by poverty. We had seen that money was so scarce that she had a hard time keeping an adequate supply of light bulbs, toilet paper, or roach control. She said, "When I had my first child, I would buy groceries very carefully and plan all my meals. When I had my second, I was still outlining a week's menu at a time. By the time I got the twins, I just started cooking in the morning until nobody was hungry anymore and then started again for lunch."

Poverty is not only grinding because one has to do without so many things; a poor person also can be worn down by other people's attitudes. With anger in her voice, this friend described an argument she had with a teacher. Because a little boy—not one of our friend's—had come to school with a patch on his pants, the teacher did not want him to sing in the school program, while our friend had strongly objected to this teacher's decision.

We were aware of the crime activities common in our friend's neighborhood, of the school drop-out rate and unemployment, of the discrimination she and her kids perceived and experienced in different places. The reality of that knowledge was not brought home to us until one day when our friend became reflective as she looked at her small sleeping sons and sighed. She had not read the statistics about how many young African-American men in this country die early, live in constant poverty, are unemployed, or spend time in jail, but she knew the truth behind the sociologists' findings. So she sighed again and said, "I wonder which one will be dead by the time he's twenty."

From this mother's point of view, her environment was a given; she didn't feel she could influence it or craft a change in her life. Only through some kind of strong lifeline thrown to her in the mire of violence and poverty in which she found herself—a lifeline she trusted because of a relationship with the one who was extending it—would she be able to hope that all of her sons would survive.

Any solution that helps someone like this woman will probably involve us caring about her in practical ways. It will involve sharing some of our increased church giving with her to meet specific goals and needs in the context of a developing friendship. What cannot be expected to work is depending solely on a bureaucratic system that keeps "the poor" at a safe distance. Of course, the ultimate key to changing a whole life, whether the person is rich or poor, has to do with opening oneself to God and trusting him to renew the way we think and feel and act. When God wanted to tell us about *his* solution, he came in the person of Jesus Christ. Therefore, if we want our neighbors to know they have alternatives, it hardly seems right only to send them anonymous caregiving. However good a program may be, we cannot get away from the fact that an important element of God's plan is for us to share ourselves as individuals.

A Case Study in "Justice for All"

Establishing personal relationships with those less fortunate than ourselves can challenge the complacency in our lives and motivate us to apply whatever power and resources we have available to help our new friends. Long gone are the informal networks which existed when a majority of people were poor. Then, relatives or neighbors who "made it" would forward used clothes, financial help or even job opportunities to the "poor cousins." Now, with the poor a minority, poverty can become self-perpetuating, especially in our cities. The poor tend to be "ghetto-ized" and otherwise isolated from the rest of the population. That sort of anonymity provides a convenient excuse for those of us not willing to become personally involved with the problems of poverty in our society. More than ever before, the have-nots are acquainted only with each other and are strangers to the mainstream citizenry.

In 1980, when we moved into a low-income housing project on Halloween, we felt as if we were moving into foreign territory. We would be the only whites in three complexes that totaled 230 units, an area that was categorized by the local police as having one of the highest crime rates in Champaign-Urbana. We moved there after some spiritual struggles about yielding to what we felt God's will to be. (We consider ourselves to be more stubborn in our determination to follow God than endowed with any other-worldly saintliness.) When we came to heartfelt agreement to move in, we had no immediate great purpose in mind. It was just that many of the people we were serving through *empty tomb* lived there, and it made sense to live among them, to experience one part of life as they did.

Because we worked at *empty tomb* and were therefore already known among these new neighbors, the transition was perhaps not as difficult as it might have been if we had been complete strangers. Still, there are people in the housing project to this day who won't speak to us. It is true that there are only a few of these people. Many of our neighbors have made a point to be friendly, and one comforted us by pointing out that there are people in the complex who won't speak to her either. Yet, this experience of being in the minority—and wondering if we are being treated as individuals or merely as stereotypes—has been unsettling.

A major challenge arrived in early 1981 when we found our first-floor apartment flooded on Palm Sunday. We reported to the management that water used to put out a fire in a neighbor's apartment had also flooded ours. No, they said, it was not water from the fire hoses. We then suggested that since there had also been a lot of rain, the storm sewers must have backed up. No, the apartment staff responded, it wasn't rainwater either.

We were running out of alternatives. "What was it?" we asked.

We were told that in the ten apartment buildings in this particular complex, there had been the ongoing problem of sanitary sewers backing up on people's floors. Did we remember that frayed spot on the hall carpet in our apartment? (Actually, at some level, we had accepted this as authentic ghetto decor.) "Well," the staff went on, "that spot rotted from the frequent sewer flooding."

When we went back to the apartment to check, we found traces of toilet paper around the standpipe in the furnace room. John had a nightmare about rats crawling up that pipe, and Sylvia now understood the series of gastrointestinal infections she had experienced since moving in. Just think of all the babies who had learned to crawl in that stuff! After we got over the first shock, we tried to figure out what to do.

We talked to our neighbors about the situation. Yes, indeed, one neighbor told us, the back-ups had happened as long as she had been there; she had moved in a decade before, soon after the apartments had opened. The tenants' council president felt she had exhausted every avenue of redress, as she had contacted the U.S. Department of Housing and Urban Development

(HUD), which had taken possession when the apartments went into default years earlier, as well as city and local agencies.

Because we believed that society did not work this way, we somewhat smugly placed a phone call to HUD's regional office in Chicago. An official listened to the problem and promised to get back to us in two days. When he called back, he sounded elated. "I told you we could solve this," he announced. Our confidence in "the system" was shaken, however, when he described the solution: HUD would "replace all the first-floor carpets with tiles so the overflows would be easier to clean up." (HUD actually used taxpayers' money for this "solution" some months later.)

Realizing this person did not grasp the seriousness of the situation, we made an appointment with a different regional HUD official to whom we were referred. Surely, we told him, he did not really understand the situation the tenants were facing. We had been advised through some members of supporting churches, who were also civil engineers at the university, that we needed diagnostic tests to find out where the problems lay. No doubt this official would be happy to provide the funds to conduct the testing and thus pave the way to solving the problem in a mutually satisfying way—or so we thought.

This official, this time an African-American, listened patiently to our presentation. He then sat forward in his chair and said, "I'm not going to give you the money for a study and I'll tell you why. I'm not going to pay good money for a study, only to find out that it's the tenants making problems for themselves. Those people eat more chicken in one week than you do in a year, and they just stuff the grease down the drain."

Our eyes popped open both mentally and physically. Could this man have really said that? Since we were the only white residents, we knew what he meant by "those people." He apparently felt so secure in his bureaucratic enclave that he didn't even try to hide his incredibly biased opinions from us.

We returned to Champaign emotionally older but much wiser. At this point we went out to the churches who were supporting our other works and explained the situation. Because many of these people were as horrified as we were, we were able to bring into play the informal networks we had available because we were educated and white and working in the broader community through *empty tomb*. One friend offered to introduce us to a person in a position to help us, whom he knew because of contact through their daughters' Brownie troop. A woman sitting next to us during a church potluck was a city official. We were also promised introductions to church members who were experts in related fields and could advise us.

There came a dramatic moment at a city council meeting soon afterward. Before approaching the council for money to do the drain testing, we had sent out the word through the churches and invited anyone who could come to join us in support. Some of our neighbors showed up, despite feeling vulnerable because their rent was being subsidized. When Sylvia spoke to the council, the first response was a suggestion to study our proposal for a grant, which would probably mean it would disappear as a neglected agenda item. Sylvia noted that, yes, she was speaking on behalf of her own apartment as well as for her neighbors in the complex. But, she went on, concern about the unhealthy living conditions forced on these residents of Champaign had a broader scope than the fate of the people trapped in horrible conditions at Fourth and Bradley. She then invited anyone who had come to the meeting because of concern about these sewers to stand. Over sixty people stood up, the vast majority not people of color! The council looked carefully at those who were stating their support, and who obviously represented all parts of Champaign—and voted the money that night.

The details of the struggle waged over the next three years to convince HUD to fix the sewers would take too long to tell here, and it is still painful to reflect on all the details. Suffice it to say that the tests the city paid for showed that the sewer lines had been installed incorrectly. Instead of flowing through sloped lines, the sewage was settling because the lines were virtually horizontal. When HUD contested these results, there were petitions and meetings and more tests and letter-writing campaigns. Both U.S. senators from Illinois and our congressional representative got involved and were very helpful. The local newspaper provided news coverage and editorial support, while the local television stations sent reporters to cover press conferences and other related events. HUD resisted and resisted, but finally provided the private company that eventually purchased the apartments with enough money to fix the sewers in seven of the ten buildings.

What a terrible experience! And to think that our neighbors had lived in these conditions for almost a decade before we ever found out about them! Yet, when the issue was brought to their attention, church members throughout the community rallied around their neighbors in need and acted nobly. All the resources these capable people had access to were successfully commandeered to right this grave injustice.

The fact remains that, for almost ten years, little kids grew up with sewage backing up on their floors, developing a self-image that said society-at-large felt it was OK for them to have raw sewage on their floors. Few outsiders would have knowingly ignored the situation. But that's just the point—the wider church did *not* know about it! There were no effective channels of communication between the residents of the complex and the broader community. They were isolated in their poverty until we stumbled in because of our faith in Jesus.

Making a Difference

We are convinced that setting up relationships between Christians with resources to share and people in need, both Christian and non-Christian, provides the most effective answer to poverty in our society. If we keep our neighbors at a distance, we cannot really understand the situations they are facing and thus cannot work with them to find long-term solutions.

Who could have guessed that one HUD official would think money spent on a cosmetic change would satisfy people facing a health risk or that another HUD official in a position to help would be prejudiced against people of his own race? Who could have guessed that the pipes were laid wrong when the project was first built? There would be no way to discover these facts without getting personally involved. The only way for the residents of the sewage-flooded apartments to solve their problem was to join with concerned people throughout the community. No pat answers suggested themselves; it took a cooperative effort to "make the system work."

Cooperative relationships—which include an element of sharing a portion of our increased church giving—are the key to providing an alternative to the isolation that keeps some people bound in poverty and others uninformed about how they are unwittingly contributing to the hostile environment. Mutual trust, on both sides of the partnership, needs to grow out of the interactions. If one or both people already trust God and the saving work of Christ, the power of the Holy Spirit will also come into play. Even then, some people in need are so enmeshed in the bonds of the poverty they've experienced— and some financially better-off people are so uncritically com-

mitted to their preconceptions about both the poor and themselves—that the partnership never really takes off. But it can.
And success is more likely when there is genuine caring.

We should also bring all of our creativity to bear in such relationships. If Christians began to give 10 percent of their
incomes, it is estimated at least $15 billion more could be avail-
able to help our local neighbors in need. Some of this might be
used for immediate problems. But we should not rule out scholarships or supplementing minimum wage jobs, or even expanding the job market by subsidizing new job opportunities.

There are probably many organizations in your community
that are in touch with people in need. Your congregation may
already work with such a group. If no existing organization
provides the opportunity for longer-term involvement with a
particular family, where structured financial sharing can take
place in a supervised context and the friendship can be nur-
tured as experienced support staff look on, there are other ways
to be involved with the poor. Volunteering in your congregation's outreach activities is one of the best ways to start.

Being a good neighbor can also be as simple as extending
yourself. One person we know became friends with a woman
as the result of a referral concerning an elaborate dollhouse a
church youth group had made. When members of the youth
group and our friend delivered the doll house to the designated
family, it was apparent that the mother was pregnant. It also
became clear, through casual conversation, that the mother had
nothing prepared for the expected baby, since she had spent all
her money trying to keep the rest of her children clothed and
fed. Our friend organized a baby shower at church and continued to stay interested in the family after the baby was born. A
long-term friendship blossomed. As Dear Abby likes to say, "To
find a friend, be one."

6

The Sky's the Limit!

Outlining a Plan of Action

*I*n the previous chapters we have considered the abundant resources that have become available to most people in America during the past several decades. The good news about these funds is that they are of sufficient quantity to make a real impact on the horrible living conditions facing many of our global neighbors. Millions of these people have never had the opportunity to hear that God loves them so much that he sent his only begotten Son. Many of them also live in such dire poverty that they have no alternative but to helplessly watch their children die. These are families we can stand with and help. Yet, even while we direct more resources overseas, we should have plenty to help our needy neighbors at home and still maintain the current programs of our congregations.

We have also explored the idea of an area-to-area strategy of sharing. The Yoking Map is a way to match Christians in the United States with people all over the world. We believe that this innovative matching process can effectively challenge church members throughout our land to rise to their full potential as we enter the next millennium with a sense of confidence in our ability to make a difference.

The personal experiences that resulted from following through on the matching idea made a huge impact on our hearts and minds. Faceless statistics were transformed into individual stories that mattered. Our global neighbors are *individuals* whom God challenges us to love as carefully and creatively as we manage to love ourselves.

The area of domestic need was considered by drawing on our work in Illinois. Becoming friends with individual members of groups different from our own seems to be the most positive strategy available for approaching poverty at home. The delightful part of this idea is that it brings the kind of joy to both giver and receiver that cannot be measured by any worldly counting system.

Having considered all these topics, we hope you are ready to ask yourself, "Where do we go from here?"

What *You* Can Do

We hope that one conclusion you have come to is that you have the ability and desire to make a difference! If you feel more affluent at the end of this book than you did when you first started reading, we have succeeded in one part of our task. It is meaningless to always compare yourself with people above you on the ladder of success. You can never be satisfied that way, for it only constantly encourages your appetite for more. Christians need to take on more of God's perspective and look at those who have far less than we have. Suddenly, what we have seems like an incredible amount! "Enough" takes on a different meaning when we consider people who don't have anything.

Increase Your Giving

If you really want to "love your neighbor," start giving more of your money away. And do it now! Putting it off will only make it harder. Go straight to 10 percent in one leap if at all possible. If not, begin to increase by regular amounts. If nothing else, plan to increase your giving by 1 percent a year. However, since this drags out the process, your enthusiasm might fade. We know one young woman who set a goal of increasing her giving by 1 percent of her income each month until she reached 10 percent. The last time we talked with her about it, she said she was making progress, even though it was a little rough.

If you already give 10 percent, good for you! But we're not going to let you off that easily. Have you considered the graduated tithe?[1] Most likely the more you earn, the greater percentage of your income is "surplus" that you can give away. Following Jesus involves stretching and striving to get in the best possible spiritual shape we can. Like the athlete who constantly tries to break an existing record, we need to be working on higher and higher goals.

Join Key Church Committees

When we talk about giving more money away, we assume that you will be giving that money to your congregation. There is a related responsibility that comes with your increased generosity, and that is the commitment to work through the committees of your church.

We would strongly urge you to follow your money through the congregational channels. Be sure that it is expanding the budget for mission projects, both domestic and overseas. On one level, churches are Christ's body on earth. However, on another level, they are very human institutions. If we give a church some extra money, there is a strong temptation to keep it for our own comfort. We are giving more to our church, we proudly tell ourselves, and then we recarpet the sanctuary and add cushions to the pews. Or we build gymnasiums and elaborate fellowship halls, until all we have really done is erect edifices that appear very much like country clubs.

Giving money is the necessary first step, but seeing that it gets distributed on behalf of the needy may be just as hard. Inquire about what mission projects your congregation is already committed to. Participate in education activities your missions committee plans. Bring your creativity and enthusiasm and interest to the effort to broaden the province of missions beyond the members of the committee to every household in the church. You might ask to join the committee or at least volunteer to serve as support personnel. You can also suggest an area-to-area focus for your congregation, referring to the Yoking Map on pp. 148–49. Your district or regional denominational office can provide information about mission activities in your yoked country.

There is another committee you can join that seems somewhat unrelated to missions, but it is one we would strongly recommend if you are serious about increasing the mission outreach of your church. That is the finance or budget committee. In our work with different churches, we have found that often the real power in the congregation rests with this committee. Parishioners can be extremely enthusiastic and want to try all kinds of projects. But, when it comes down to it, if the people on the finance committee are not sold on the idea, they have lots of ways, including plain inaction, to curb any such activities and channel available funds in other directions.

Finance committees often see themselves as conducting the real business of the church. Concerns about building maintenance, property acquisition, ongoing expenses, and other practical matters of the church program give the people in charge of the budget a great deal of authority. In some congregations, they are not afraid to use that power if they feel a group of members is taking the church too far out of its previously defined path. These people do give remarkable service to their congregation, and many care deeply about making the church the best it can be, but the temptation to *preserve* rather than *serve* can become a stumbling block to creativity and change.

You will have to do a lot of homework if you sit on this committee. Although you must be prepared to get involved in a lot of details, you will be in the valuable position of constantly keeping the broader vision of the church on the committee's agenda, which will benefit everyone in the long run.

You should approach any type of committee work as a challenge to your ingenuity and patience. After doing extensive interviews among congregations, we have come to one alarming conclusion: In terms of money and stewardship, there are some church patterns that one could almost term "dysfunctional." Because most people understand that the mission of the church is to serve others, this purpose will often be mentioned and considered in worship services and special seminars. But when it comes to making service and outreach a priority, there seems to be such incredible inertia that efforts tend to fall apart from exhaustion! We talked to a pastor who said one of his parishioners told him she joined strategic church committees specifically to make sure that nothing really changed! Other church leaders have expressed the feeling that the whole area of money was sometimes used to control the pastor or the direction of the church—or both. Individual members had certain agendas that would never be submitted for a vote but were made clear by whether these individuals' contributions were given or withheld.

You will also need to be very definite about whether you actually want to challenge your congregation to give more money and be increasingly involved with missions. We pointed out in chapter 3 that congregations were unlikely to increase mission giving if they did not feel a mutual accountability with the denominational agencies. It is also true that individual members need to feel that the congregation at large is open to their input. We have observed one common pattern often cited among congregations: A few families give most of the money. Church leaders often complain about this fact, implying that more people should be sharing in the support of the church. In reality, those same families may well covet (however unconsciously) the influence that a high level of contributions automatically gives them, and they can actually feel threatened when others join them in strongly supporting the church.

It takes a certain stubbornness and a lot of committed love, prayer, and the power of the Holy Spirit to break through these negative patterns of giving. "Is the effort worth it?" you might ask. We would counter with another question: "Do we really have any choice?" The church is Christ's body on earth. We must exert all our best efforts to make it the creative tool for evangelism, service, and the glorification of God that it was designed to be.

You may have heard the following story, which was told to us by W. H. Donaldson, a retired minister who has had a deep influence on our lives. He describes Jesus returning to heaven from earth, being surrounded by eager saints who have gone before. One asks him, "But if you are here, who will carry on the work down there?"

Jesus replies, "I have left behind my church to do it."

At this news, there is a worried murmur among the crowd. Finally one brave soul asks, "But Master, do you think that was wise? What if they don't carry on? Then what will you do?"

Jesus looks rather sadly at those gathered around him and shakes his head as he says, "I have no other plan, my friends. I have no other plan."

A Pilot Project

We are currently working on a pilot project with a set of congregations. Our hope is to design a practical structure that will help congregations with their efforts to become better channels of service to others.

Our project is named "The National Money for Missions Program."™ The first phase turned out to be an effort to define a congregational baseline for stewardship. The eight brave congregations involved in this phase of the model were venturing out into a previously undefined area. In each case, the administrative board or council of the congregation had voted to participate in the study. The agreed-upon goal was to first develop a sustainable budget for the congregation and then try to raise funds *beyond* this budget to supplement current mission support. The congregational leadership agreed with the basic structure of the program: The majority of funds raised beyond the defined budget would go through denominational channels, with the international funds directed to programs supported by the denomination in the yoked country. Another significant part of the surplus funds would be used to help one or more specific local families in need. A member of each congregation was designated to assist the pastor with stewardship and mission education.

The participating congregational leadership found it difficult to communicate these revised expectations to their church members. While everyone agreed *in theory* that increased missions giving was a commendable goal, actually moving in that direction required a lot of effort on the practical level.

Nevertheless, at the end of the first year, several of the congregations reported markedly more positive attitudes toward stewardship among their parishioners. The project catalyzed dialogues which focused on defining the common agenda of the congregation. This proved to be a very constructive activity. One congregation raised funds beyond its budget in the first year. Six of the original eight congregations moved into the second year of the pilot with clear expectations of making deeper changes in the way members approached the whole topic of stewardship and missions funding.

The second phase of the pilot is designed to introduce this revised program structure in several congregations, based on what was learned from the first phase. After the second phase is underway, the timetable calls for a general expansion into a large number of churches. All these steps are geared to develop a practical, reproducible program that can be implemented in any congregation that seriously wants to adjust its giving patterns. We have concluded that this plan would not be useful to those congregations that want to alter the status quo only slightly, raising more money only to fund a particular building project or temporarily support a special cause. Rather, The National Money for Missions Program is more like a weight-loss program or addiction counseling; it requires a deep commitment on the part of the participants to address the fundamental changes required for long-term improvement.

We remain convinced that people in congregations want to make a difference in Jesus' name. We hope The National Money for Missions Program will be a practical means toward that end.

Missions for the Rest of Us

If you feel the call to go to another country in full-time mission service, we encourage you to do so. That challenge is a precious opportunity. With all the changes taking place around the globe, you will be at the cutting edge of history. It is now more likely than ever that you can work side by side with people in other countries to establish meaningful relationships and affirm the true meaning of Christian oneness on very practical terms. However, you must never forget your responsibility to educate folks back in the United States about your work. This communication link is almost as important as the service you will be able to render abroad.

If, instead, you feel the call to a career in a helping agency in the United States, we also affirm your noble purpose. Standing with people across town as they face difficult situations is a wonderful way to spend your life. While you seek to help people who have limited material resources, remember to facilitate ways for those who cannot join you full-time to cooperate in your work.

On the other hand, even if you don't feel called overseas or to full-time service at home, let us assure you that you are still called to missions! You are part of an important support network, the sinews that hold the body together, the blood that distributes life-sustaining oxygen where it is needed, the bones around which the rest of the structure is built.

Once you open yourself fully to Jesus and his kingdom, you will want to respond to a vast and glorious calling. Then your occupation will not only be a way to honor God by responsibly carrying out your duties. It will also be a means of earning resources by which you can accomplish miraculous results if you share them in love and servanthood. Your very residence in a country with religious freedom, advanced communication methods, and an efficient transportation system means that you need not be limited by the fact that you are not working on these matters full-time. If mission efforts are to assume their rightful place in the center of the church's agenda, you have a vital role to play.

We are living in exciting times. We are living in dangerous times. We are living in the times that God has designed. Let us respond to these times with enthusiasm and hope and creativity. The challenge is great, but the power of our Lord makes us equal to the task set before us.

> Now to him who is able to do immeasurably more than all we ask or imagine, according to his power that is at work within us, to him be glory in the church and in Christ Jesus through-out all generations, for ever and ever! Amen (Eph. 3:20–21).

The Yoking Map™

The map that follows on pages 148–49 is described in chapter 4, pages 79–84.

The Yoking Map™

Notes

Chapter 1: *Bread from Jesus*

1. "Yearly Report for the Bread from Jesus Fund, Period October 1986 to August 1987" (Champaign, Ill.: Diaconia of Brazil for *empty tomb, inc.,* Fall 1987), 2.

2. Ibid., 2–3. "Approximately 40% of the deaths of children under one year of age are caused by infectious and parasitic disease, while in the South of Brazil the rate for the same is only 8.1%."

According to *The State of the World's Children 1988* (New York: UNICEF, December 1987) pp. 2–3, diarrheal diseases, measles, acute respiratory infectious malaria, and tetanus are the major causes of death of children under five throughout all developing countries. Diarrheal diseases and measles are also cited as major causes of malnutrition.

3. Sound cassette interview with Inez Brito de Siqueira, conducted, translated, and transcribed by Diaconia, Recife, Brazil (Champaign, Ill.: *empty tomb, inc.,* 1987).

Chapter 2: *Abounding Grace*

1. James P. Grant, *The State of the World's Children 1988* (New York: Oxford University Press, 1987), 57.

2. Ruth Leger Sivard, *World Military and Social Expenditures 1987–88* (Washington, D.C.: World Priorities, 1987), 28.

3. James P. Grant, *The State of the World's Children 1987* (New York: Oxford University Press, 1987), 109. The 136 million is a minimum number, since the 1950 child death total was double the 1986 total. We have used a constant 1986 total of 13.6 million child deaths as estimated by UNICEF in this comparison.

4. James P. Grant, *The State of the World's Children 1982–83* (New York, UNICEF, 1983), 1.

5. *World Press Review,* January 1, 1980, 56; Grant, *The State of the World's Children 1987,* 36.

6. James W. Reapsome, "Great Commission Deadline," *Christianity Today*, January 15, 1988, 24.

7. Donald McNeill, Douglas Morrison, and Henri Nouwen, *Compassion* (New York: Doubleday, 1983), 53.

8. An earlier verson of chart 1916–89 first appeared in *The Midas Trap*, a Christianity Today Series Book.

9. John Ronsvalle and Sylvia Ronsvalle, *The State of Church Giving, through 1989*, rev. ed. (Champaign, Ill.: *empty tomb, inc.*, 1991).

10. Sylvia Nasar, "Do We Live as Well as We Used to?" *Fortune*, September 14, 1987, 42.

11. W. Dayton Roberts and John A. Siewert, eds., *The Mission Handbook, 14th ed.* (Monrovia, Calif.: Missions Advanced Research and Communication Center, 1989), 51.

12. Inquiries indicate that there is no central reporting source for U.S. Catholic giving statistics. According to p. 29 of the *1989–90 Mission Handbook*, (Washington, D.C.: U.S. Catholic Mission Association, 1989), the total number of Catholic missionaries has been decreasing since the late 1960s. The number of Catholics sent out from the church in the U.S. in 1987 was 6,073. This is in contrast to an estimated 40,221 career Protestant workers reported in *The Mission Handbook, 14th ed.* It may be reasonable to assume that U.S. Catholic agencies' income for overseas ministries would not exceed $300 million.

13. The 37% figure is derived from two sources. Over the past decade, Gallup polls indicate that an average of 41% of the U.S. population attended a weekly worship service as noted in the *Yearbook of American and Canadian Churches*, ed. Constant H. Jacquet (Nashville: Abingdon Press, 1989), 277. According to calculations based on data from the *World Christian Encyclopedia*, ed. David Barrett (New York: Oxford University Press, 1982), 711–28, somewhat over 90% of those affiliated with religious organizations in the U.S. are related to historically Christian organizations.

14. Barrett, *World Christian Encyclopedia*, 711.

15. Levi Keidel, "The Whole Gospel, God's Interest for Our Wholeness," sound cassette of a talk delivered at the Festival of World Mission, First Mennonite Church, Newton, Kansas, March 3, 1984.

16. Jerry White, *The Church and the Parachurch* (Portland, Oreg.: Multnomah Press, 1983), 103.

17. *"Christianity Today* Surveys the Top TV Preachers," *Christianity Today*, October 16, 1987, 48–49; and Randy Frame, et al., "Surviving the Slump," *Christianity Today*, February 3, 1989, 34. From these two sources, 1986 estimates for 13 major television evangelists suggest that total receipts were $649 million. An estimate for total religious giving from *Giving USA 1989*, ed. Nathan Weber (American Association of Fund-Raising Counsel, New York, 1989), 80, was adjusted by a figure for historically Christian adherents.

18. James P. Grant, *The State of the World's Children, 1989* (New York: Oxford University Press, 1989), 65.

19. Luther P. Powell, *Money and the Church* (New York: Association Press, 1962), 15.

20. Ibid., 30.

21. Ibid., 46.

22. Ibid., 70–77.

23. Ibid., 105–122.

24. Ibid., 140–142.

25. Ibid., 123–147.

26. Ibid., 21–22.

27. Jacques Ellul, *Money and Power* (Downers Grove, Ill.: Inter-Varsity Press, 1984), 75–77, 110–111.

28. James P. Grant, *The State of the World's Children 1991* (New York: Oxford University Press, 1991), 37–47.

29. Kevin G. Dyer, "I Saw Missionaries Cry," *The Christian Reader,* vol. 6, no. 11 (February-March, 1968), 54–55.

30. Elmore Clyde, "Compassion: Caring for the Whole Person," *Light and Life,* February 1988, 6.

31. Roberts and Siewert, eds., *The Mission Handbook, 14th ed.,* 51. Note: Although the $1.73 billion figure is under a 1988 heading in *The Mission Handbook* the questionnaire used to compile the information requests 1987 data from the responding agencies (see the Appendices, page 491 of *The Mission Handbook*).

32. Sylvia Porter, "Tips Given on Selecting Florist," *The Champaign-Urbana News-Gazette,* April 3, 1985, B-8.

33. Pet Food Institute statistics quoted by Cotten Timberlake, "Billion Dollar Business," Associated Press in *The Champaign-Urbana News-Gazette,* June 21, 1985, B-9.

34. Lawrence Kilman, "Ordinance Worries Chemical Lawn-Care Firms," Associated Press in *The Champaign-Urbana News-Gazette,* April 4, 1985, D-3.

35. A National Association of Hosiery Manufacturers statistic quoted by Robert M. Andrews, "Nylon Stockings: Celebrating a 50-year Run," Associated Press in *The Champaign-Urbana News-Gazette,* January 17, 1988, E-5.

36. A SAMI-Burke Market Research statistic quoted by "Food for Microwaves Makes for Marketing Battle," New York Times Service in *The Champaign-Urbana News-Gazette,* Feb. 21, 1988, C-4.

37. Bill Barol, "Where All the Quarters Go," *Newsweek,* December 5, 1988, 78.

38. Jerry Adler, et al., "The Nintendo Kid," *Newsweek,* March 6, 1989, 67.

39. "Skin-Care Claims: The Latest Wrinkle," *Newsweek,* April 18, 1989, 86.

40. Ron Givens, et al., "Hail the Size of Golf Balls," *Newsweek,* August 8, 1988, 71.

41. Eric N. Berg of New York Times Service, in "Wrigley Doubles Its Income Pleasure with Single Devotion," *The Champaign-Urbana News-Gazette,* November 27, 1988, C-3.

42. An Electronics Industry Association statistic quoted in a Knight-Ridder article appearing as "Sales Soar for Stereo Sytems That Make 'the Cars Go Boom,'" *The Champaign-Urbana News-Gazette,* July 5, 1989, S-6.

43. National Spa and Pool Institute statistic quoted by Robert J. Samuelson, "The American Sports Mania," *Newsweek,* September 4, 1989, 49.

44. Marco R. della Cava, "Candy Industry's Growth Stale," *USA Today,* October 31, 1989, 6B.

45. Marketdata Enterprises figure quoted in "Diets Incorporated," *Newsweek,* September 11, 1989, 56.

46. Samuelson, *Newsweek,* 49.

47. Ibid., a National Sporting Goods Association statistic.

48. Ibid., a National Marine Manufacturers Association statistic, with estimate by Samuelson.

49. Annetta Miller with Vern E. Smith, "The Soda War Fizzes Up," *Newsweek,* March 19, 1990, 38.

50. Associated Press article entitled "Hollywood Has Best Summer: $2.05 billions," *The Champaign-Urbana News-Gazette,* September 9, 1989, C-9.

51. Robert Whereatt, "As the Stakes Rise, So Do Fears of Fallout," *Minneapolis-St. Paul Star Tribune,* September 23, 1990, 1A.

52. Washington Cosmetology Association Nail Fashion Committee statistic quoted in an Associated Press story appearing as "Nailing Down a Million-dollar Business with Diamonds, Pearls and Holograms," *The Champaign-Urbana News-Gazette,* October 2, 1989, A-6.

Chapter 3: *The Vision Unfolds*

1. Jacques Ellul, *Money and Power* (Downers Grove, Ill.: Inter-Varsity Press, 1984), 94–96.

2. The Princeton Religion Research Center found that "half the nation's population believes that religion is losing its influence in American life . . ." as observed in *Giving USA 1989,* ed. Nathan Weber (New York: AAFRC Trust for Philanthropy, 1989), 81.

3. The Barna Research Group, *The Church Today: Insightful Statistics and Commentary* (Glendale, Calif.: The Barna Research Group, 1990), 25.

4. Juvenal, in *Satires, I,* writes, ". . . luxury, more deadly than war, broods over the city and avenges a conquered world." *Familiar Quotations by John Bartlett,* ed. Emily Morison Beck, et al. (Boston: Little, Brown, 1980), 122.

5. A. James Reichley, *Religion in American Public Life* (Washington, D.C.: The Brookings Institution, 1985), 360.

6. For example, see Commission on World Mission and Evangelism of the World Council of Churches, "Mission and Evangelism—An Ecumenical Affirmation," *International Review of Mission,* vol. LXXI, no. 284 (October, 1982): "There is also a tragic coincidence that most of the world's poor have not heard the Good News of the Gospel of Jesus Christ; or they could not receive it, because it was not recognized as Good News in the way in which it was brought. This is a double injustice: they are victims of oppression of an unjust economic order or an unjust political distribution of power, and at the same time they are deprived of the

knowledge of God's special care for them. To announce the Good News to the poor is to begin to render the justice due to them" (p. 440).

7. Ralph Winter, "The Unreached World," *Target Earth*, ed. Frank Kaleb Jansen (Pasadena, Calif.: Global Mapping International, with University of the Nations, Hawaii, 1989), 140.

8. "The Report of the World Food Council on the Work of Its Thirteenth Session, 8–11 June, 1987" (New York: United Nations General Assembly Official Records: Forty-Second Session Supplement No. 19 (A/42/19), 15–16.

9. James P. Grant, *The State of the World's Children 1990* (New York: Oxford University Press, 1990), 13.

10. Charles H. Fahs, *Trends in Protestant Giving* (New York: Institute of Social and Religious Research, 1929), 6.

11. Grant, *The State of the World's Children 1990*, 16.

12. David Barrett, ed., *World Christian Encyclopedia* (New York: Oxford University Press, 1982).

13. Morris David, *Measuring the Condition of the World's Poor* (New York: Pergamon Press, 1979), 20ff.

14. Population Crisis Committee, *Human Suffering Index* (Washington, D.C.: Population Crisis Committee, 1987) appearing in *Target Earth*, ed. Jansen, 88–89.

15. *The Amity Foundation 1991 Calendar* (Nanjing, PRC: The Amity Foundation, 1991).

16. *Amity Foundation Newsletter, no. 6* (Winter, 1987–88), 4.

Chapter 4: *China, Hello!*

1. G. Thompson Brown, *Christianity in the People's Republic of China* (Louisville, Ky.: Westminster-John Knox Press, 1986), 9, 10.

2. Marwyn Samuels, "Disillusionment with China?" *Connections*, Syracuse University, vol. 4, no. 1 (December 1989): 2.

3. State Statistical Bureau, PRC, *Statistical Yearbook of China 1985* (Beijing: China Statistical Information and Consultancy Service Centre, 1985), 186.

4. Gao Shi, "Village Switches On to Alternative Energy," *China Daily*, June 3, 1986, 1.

5. *The Constitution of the People's Republic of China*, adopted on December 4, 1982, by the Fifth National People's Congress of the People's Republic of China at its Fifth Session (Beijing: Foreign Languages Press, 1983), 25.

6. For an overview of the history of Christianity in China, see Brown, *Christianity in the People's Republic of China*, 1986.

7. David Barrett, ed., *World Christian Encyclopedia* (New York: Oxford University Press, 1982), 231.

8. Brown, *Christianity in the People's Republic of China*, 36.

9. Ibid., 134.

10. Ibid., 163.

11. Ibid., 165.

12. Ibid., 86.

Chapter 6: *The Sky's the Limit*

1. For a discussion of the graduated tithe, see chapter seven of Ronald J. Sider, *Rich Christians in an Age of Hunger* (Downers Grove, Ill.: Inter-Varsity Press, 1979).